Tan Tien
Chi Kung

Tan Tien Chi Kung

Foundational Exercises for Empty Force and Perineum Power

Mantak Chia

Destiny Books
Rochester, Vermont

Destiny Books
One Park Street
Rochester, Vermont 05767
www.InnerTraditions.com

Destiny Books is a division of Inner Traditions International

Originally published in Thailand in 2002 by Universal Tao Publications under the
title *Tan Tien Chi Kung: Empty Force, Perineum Power and the Second Brain*

LIBRARY OF CONGRESS CATALOGING-IN-PUBLICATION DATA
Chia, Mantak, 1944-
Tan Tien Chi Kung : foundational exercises for empty force and perineum power
/ Mantak Chia.
p. cm.
ISBN 0-89281-195-1
1. Qi gong. 2. Abdominal exercises. 3. Perineum. I. Title.
RA781.8.C4696 2004
613.7'1886—dc22
2004010281

Printed and bound in China

10   9   8   7   6   5   4   3   2   1

Text design by Priscilla Baker
This book was typeset in Janson with Present, Futura, and Diotima as
the display typefaces

Contents

Acknowledgments

The Universal Tao Publications staff involved in the preparation and production of this book extend our gratitude to the many generations of Taoist masters who have passed on their special lineage, in the form of an oral transmission, over thousands of years. We thank Taoist Master I Yun (Yi Eng) for his openness in transmitting the formulas of Taoist Inner Alchemy.

We offer our eternal gratitude to our parents and teachers for their many gifts to us. Remembering them brings joy and satisfaction to our continued efforts in presenting the Universal Tao System. As always, their contribution has been crucial in presenting the concepts and techniques of the Universal Tao.

We wish to thank the thousands of unknown men and women of the Chinese healing arts who developed many of the methods and ideas presented in this book. We offer our gratitude to Master Lao Kang Wen for sharing his healing techniques.

We wish to thank Susan Bridle and Vickie Trihy for editing this new edition of *Tan Tien Chi Kung* and the following people who contributed to the first edition: Colin Campbell for his editorial work, writing contributions, and research; Jean Chilton for her editorial contributions; our Senior Instructors Felix Senn and Annette Derksen, as well as Riki Robinson and Sarina Stone, for their insightful contributions; and Spafford Ackerly and Joost Kuitenbrouwer for their technical editing and clear writing.

Thanks to Juan Li for the use of his beautiful and visionary paintings illustrating Taoist esoteric practices. Special thanks also to Raruen Keawapadung, computer graphics; Saysunee Yongyod, photographer; and Udon Jandee, illustrator.

Putting Tan Tien Chi Kung into Practice

The practices described in this book have been used successfully for thousands of years by Taoists trained by personal instruction. Readers should not undertake these practices without receiving personal instruction from a certified instructor of the Universal Tao System because some of these practices, if done improperly, may cause injury or result in health problems. This book is intended to supplement individual training with a Universal Tao instructor and to serve as a reference guide for these practices. Anyone who undertakes these practices on the basis of this book alone does so entirely at his or her own risk. Universal Tao instructors can be located at our websites: www.universal-tao.com or www.taoinstructors.org.

The meditations, practices, and techniques described herein are *not* intended to be used as an alternative or substitute for professional medical treatment and care. If a reader is suffering from a mental or emotional disorder, he or she should consult with an appropriate professional health care practitioner or therapist. Such problems should be corrected before one starts training.

This book does not attempt to give any medical diagnosis, treatment, prescription, or remedial recommendation in relation to any human disease, ailment, suffering, or physical condition whatsoever.

Chinese Medicine and Chi Kung emphasize balancing and strengthening the body so that it can heal itself. The meditations, internal exercises, and martial arts of the Universal Tao are basic approaches to this end. Follow the instructions for each exercise carefully, and do not neglect the foundations (such as the Microcosmic Orbit practice and any other supplemental exercises). Also pay special attention to the warnings and suggestions. People who have high blood pressure, heart disease, or a generally weak condition should proceed cautiously, having received prior consent from a qualified medical practitioner. People with venereal disease should not attempt any practices involving sexual energy until they are free of the condition.

The Universal Tao and its staff and instructors cannot be responsible for the consequences of any practice or misuse of the information in this book. If the reader undertakes any exercise without strictly following the instructions, notes, and warnings, the responsibility must lie solely with the reader.

 *Introduction*

TAN TIEN CHI KUNG

The Universal Tao is a practical system of self-development that enables individuals to complete the harmonious evolution of their physical, mental, and spiritual bodies. Through a series of ancient Chinese meditative and internal energy exercises, the practitioner learns to increase physical energy, release tension, improve health, practice self-defense, and gain the ability to heal oneself and others. In the process of creating a solid foundation of health and well-being in the physical body, one also creates the basis for developing one's spiritual potential.

Tan Tien Chi Kung is an important branch of Universal Tao. *Chi* means "energy" or "life force"; *kung* means "work." Traditionally, Chi Kung is the cultivation of the ability to conduct Chi for the purposes of healing. Tan Tien Chi Kung is a form of Chi Kung that particularly focuses on working with the lower Tan Tien, one of the principal energy centers of the body.

According to the Taoist view, there are three sources of Chi: cosmic Chi, universal Chi, and earth Chi. Cosmic Chi is born out of the original Chi of the Tao and literally carries the intelligence and essence of life. Guided by this intelligence, it spreads out into the universe and manifests in different densities and forms defined by the cosmic laws. This is how stars, planets, human cells, subatomic particles, and all other forms of life take form and are nourished.

Universal and earth Chi also have their genesis in the original energy of the Tao. The universal Chi is the radiating force of all galaxies, stars, and planets throughout the whole universe. It is the all-pervasive force that nourishes the life energy in all the forms of nature. The earth Chi is the third force of nature, which includes all the energies of mother earth. This force is activated by the electromagnetic field originating in the rotation of the earth. It is also integrated into all aspects of nature on our planet. The earth energy is accessed through the soles of the feet, the perineum, and the sexual organs. Earth energy nourishes the physical body. It supplies our daily life force and is one of the principal forces used to heal ourselves.

For the past five thousand years, practitioners of Chi Kung have used time-tested methods to tap into these unlimited reservoirs of Chi, greatly expanding the amount of energy available to them.

The Universal Tao system also speaks of two types of Chi operating in the human being: prenatal Chi and postnatal Chi. Prenatal Chi, which is a combination of universal Chi and Jing (generative energy/sexual essence), is inherited from the parents, and is visible as innate vitality. Postnatal Chi, which is the life force an individual cultivates in his or her lifetime, is visible as the light shining behind personality and self-awareness. To build their postnatal Chi, humans normally access Chi through food and air. Plants take the universal energies of the sun and the magnetic energies of the earth and digest and transform them, thereby making these energies available to all living beings.

Rather than connecting to this universal Chi only after it is processed through plants, however, Taoist practitioners of Chi Kung learn to go directly to the source of this primordial energy. The Taoist recognizes that human beings have a limited capacity for Chi. However, if we are able to connect with the sources of Chi within the universe, we gain an infinite capacity for Chi, and we constantly fill ourselves, within the limitations of our human nature, with the unlimited abundance of energy around us.

Tan Tien Chi Kung (also called "second brain Chi Kung" for reasons that will be discussed later) is the art of cultivating and condensing Chi in the lower Tan Tien through the Empty Force breathing practices and the Perineum Power exercises. The lower Tan Tien is the primary energy center of the body. It is the major generator and storage place for Chi energy in the body as well as the center of awareness. There are two other Tan Tiens, or energy centers, in the body: the middle Tan Tien and the upper Tan Tien. The three Tan Tiens each have specific energetic functions.

The lower Tan Tien, which is especially utilized in Tan Tien Chi Kung, is the center of the physical body and of physical strength. It is located behind and below the navel—in the triangle between the navel, the "kidney center point" (in the spine between the second and third lumbar, also called the "gate of life"), and the sexual center. For men, the sexual center is the prostate gland; for women, it lies in the top of the cervix between the ovaries.

The lower Tan Tien is also called the "medicine field" or "elixir field," as it gathers and contains the healing power of Chi. Other names for it are the "ocean of Chi," the "sea of energy," the "cauldron," and the "navel center." The use of the expressions "ocean" and "sea" refer to the wavelike quality of Chi. The expression "cauldron" refers to the function of the lower Tan Tien as the center of internal alchemy that transforms energy.

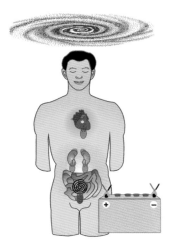

THE LOWER TAN TIEN IS LIKE A BATTERY

The lower Tan Tien serves as the source of the life force or vital force. This then becomes transformed into the more subtle Shen Chi, or spirit power/energy. Thus, throughout all Universal Tao practices, the lower Tan Tien remains the key to supplying the body and the mind with a free, uninterrupted flow of energy. Tan Tien Chi Kung is above all a practice by which the unity of what is above and below is acknowledged and honored. Through its service as a reservoir and transformer of Chi, the lower Tan Tien confirms the unity between earth and heaven in the body.

In the Universal Tao System, there is a strong emphasis on practitioners being "rooted and grounded," which refers to establishing stability both mentally and physically. Tan Tien Chi Kung is an effective method of bringing us "down to earth" and receiving the energy of the earth. It also helps us to live from our own center and be proactive instead of reactive. Tan Tien Chi Kung proposes that the source of true happiness and joy lies within our very selves and not anywhere else. The negative energies within and around us, which we may experience as obstacles to our happiness, are the "raw material" for energy transformation. Through this practice we may learn to accept and appreciate ourselves, others, and the world around us. We learn to see our own negative energies as garbage we can recycle into compost that can then serve to fortify our positive energies.

The lower Tan Tien is the place where our prenatal Chi is stored, it is the place where all the energy that we absorb and collect during the Chi Kung exercises is stored, and it is the place where denser energies are transformed into more subtle energies. In the various practices of Tan Tien Chi Kung discussed in this book, particularly the Empty Force and Perineum Power exercises, we learn to feel, strengthen, and conduct Chi through the power of the mind with particular attention to the lower Tan Tien.

UNIVERSAL TAO BASIC PRACTICES AND PREPARATION EXERCISES

In the Universal Tao System, we teach Tan Tien Chi Kung within a comprehensive framework of exercises and meditation. As a part of this system, Tan Tien Chi Kung focuses on cultivating the ability to sense, control, strengthen, and project Chi. One can easily learn the simple exercises of Tan Tien Chi Kung without doing any other Universal Tao practices, but if one truly wishes to master the art of Tan Tien Chi Kung, it is important to have a firm foundation in the basic Universal Tao practices. Therefore we suggest that you become familiar with the basic practices and exercises outlined in the first three chapters of Mantak Chia's *Taoist Cosmic Healing*. Throughout this book, we will refer periodically to these preparatory practices and will direct you to *Taoist Cosmic Healing*. We will also refer you to other Mantak Chia books that present different aspects of Chi Kung practice.

Chi and the Lower Tan Tien

CHI PRESSURE

In Tan Tien Chi Kung we learn to increase the flow of Chi in our bodies and strengthen the Chi pressure in the lower Tan Tien, organs, and fascia (connective tissue). Chi "pressure" refers to the result of condensing a large amount of energy into a small space. This is not unlike the effect of packing air into a tire until the tire becomes strong enough to safely support the weight of a heavy vehicle. "Strengthening Chi pressure" means to increase the level of Chi and to increase the internal pressure of the body so that we will be healthier and live longer. The by-product of this process is the ability to use that pressure for Chi power manipulation. Much like a living battery, we may build up and store energy (Chi). If we store enough of this energy, then we are able to use it to accomplish greater things, including the healing of our bodies. There are many ways in which to create Chi power pressure, several of which we will discuss in this book.

We can actually increase our vital energy, strengthen our organs, and promote self-healing by increasing the Chi pressure in our organs and body cavity. With increased Chi pressure, the circulatory system, lymphatic system, nervous system, and endocrine glands will all be activated, and blood, spinal fluid, and hormones will flow more easily. The practices of Tan Tien Chi Kung particularly increase pressure in the abdominal cavity, which increases the Chi pressure used to move the Chi, blood, and lymph fluid.

As we begin to increase the Chi pressure within the organs, the organs will start to gain in size, strength, and ability to store Chi energy. As the body starts to adapt to the increased amounts of pressure, it will start to be able to store more and more energy in order to release more energy. This can be likened to blowing up a large balloon. The balloon, when unfilled, is flaccid and has no pressure at all. When you start to blow up the balloon, it starts to stretch and fill up with air, and the air pressure within it increases. Our organs are very similar to that balloon, in that we can actually increase the pounds of pressure that our organs can sustain. As our Chi pressure increases and after we let the organs accommodate that new energy pressure, our body will be stronger and able to emit stronger Chi.

When people are sick, the Chi pressure in their bodies decreases and falls below the Chi pressure from outside, which is about 14.7 PSI (pounds per square inch). Sick people cannot take much pressure from outside; they become tired very quickly and irritated by people and circumstances. Life becomes a burden. A lack of Chi pressure also slows down all circulation (Chi, blood, lymph, and spinal fluid). It is a downward spiraling movement of the whole life force.

Developing the Chi pressure is one of the best practices we can use to reverse the downward spiraling movement of the quantity and quality of our life force into an upward spiraling movement. The increase of the Chi pressure in our lower Tan Tien through Tan Tien Chi Kung will enhance our healing, martial arts (Iron Shirt and Tai Chi), meditation abilities, and the art of daily living. It will also nourish our original force.

Chi pressure in the lower Tan Tien roots our body and mind. It is our grounding wire in the earth. When the Chi pressure is low, we will have no rooting. The energy in the body and mind will be unfocused and will quickly dissipate, causing overheating, headache, pain in the heart, and a distracted mind.

When you want to become a big tree, you need deep roots, which require a high Chi pressure in the lower Tan Tien. This is one of the reasons why Tan Tien Chi Kung is the foundation for Iron Shirt and Tai Chi Chi Kung. It is also important for meditation practice. The inner power in the Tan Tien helps us to regain our inner peace and stillness and our connection with the mind of the Tao.

TAN TIEN POWER

We need Chi and Chi pressure in the lower Tan Tien as a foundation for most of the Universal Tao practices, especially for Iron Shirt Chi Kung, Tai Chi Chi Kung, and meditation. The lower Tan Tien is the energy reservoir in the body. It is the place where we store the energy we generate, gather, and absorb in Chi Kung and meditation. If the energy is stored in the lower Tan Tien it can be accessed later, but if it is not stored, the Chi dissipates and cannot be used.

The lower Tan Tien is also called the "ocean of Chi." According to Chinese medical theory, once the ocean is full, it will overflow into the eight extraordinary meridians, the eight principle energy channels of the body. Once these are full, the Chi flows into the twelve ordinary meridians, each of which is associated with a particular organ. The lower Tan Tien is therefore the foundation of the entire energetic system of the body.

We usually refer to the lower abdominal area as the lower Tan Tien; this is the area that Tan Tien Chi Kung particularly works with. However, as noted previously, we actually have three Tan Tiens: the lower Tan Tien (in the abdomen, the seat of awareness), the middle Tan Tien (the heart, the seat of consciousness), and the upper Tan Tien (behind the mid-eyebrow point, the seat of Shen, or spirit). You can read more about the Tan Tiens in the Universal Tao publication *Opening the Three Tan Tiens in Six Directions*. All three Tan Tiens are used in Taoist inner alchemy. Because of their capacity to deal with a large amount of Chi, the Tan Tiens are used as a "laboratory" for inner alchemical work. Translated from the Chinese, the word *Tan* means "elixir." *Tien* means "field or place." It is the place where all the energies of our body, the earth, the universe, and nature come together to form the "pearl," the elixir of immortality, and the nourishment for our soul and spirit.

In Iron Shirt Chi Kung practice, we learn to stand effortlessly and relaxed in the "embrace the tree" position using our internal body structure and alignment or rooting. We also develop a powerful pelvic floor and centering in the lower Tan Tien. (You can learn about the practice of Iron Shirt Chi Kung in Mantak Chia's *Iron Shirt Chi Kung*.) In Tai Chi Chi Kung we learn to move this "tree," circulate the energy, and strengthen our internal power. (You can learn about the practice of Tai Chi Chi Kung in Mantak Chia's *Tai Chi Chi Kung*.) All movements in Tai Chi originate from the lower Tan Tien. This important region is responsible for control and balance, two key ingredients in proper Tai Chi execution. Additionally, the Chi generated through Chi Kung practice is stored in the lower Tan Tien.

Practicing Tan Tien Chi Kung will develop our internal and rooting power and our ability to center the body and mind. "Internal power" refers to the amount of Chi available for management. "Rooting" keeps us grounded while we experience the beginnings of intense energetic expansion. As a matter of interest, it is good to know that rooting abilities will continue to develop proportionally with internal power throughout the growth process, thus facilitating the requisite balance for handling greater levels of Chi.

It is necessary that enough energy is stored in the lower Tan Tien so that it is filled with Chi pressure and that our mind is strong and focused in the lower Tan Tien area. This will also make us more focused, stable, and balanced in daily life, and will enhance our personal power. While the lower Tan Tien is both the source and container of Chi power, the mind acts as the commander that issues orders to the lower Tan Tien for directing Chi power. In this way, we can draw energy quickly and effectively from the lower Tan Tien and direct it for healing or other purposes.

THE LOWER TAN TIEN AND THE SECOND BRAIN

Taoist masters discovered that human beings have an upper mind or brain, and a lower mind or brain. We can call the first, upper brain the "logical" brain, and the second, lower brain the "intuitive" brain. The gut, or intuitive brain, receives important messages about our bodies and the world outside and passes these messages to our logical brain. When we strive to listen effectively to our intuitive brain with our logical brain, the result is a better connection to ourselves.

The existence of the feeling and awareness brain has been scientifically proven. In 1996 Sandra Blakeslee wrote an article in the *New York Times* about the "hidden brain in the gut." It described the work of researchers who had found that the gut, or enteric nervous system, as they called it, functioned similarly to the brain. They had discovered that the large and small intestines had the same type of neurons as are found in the brain, and that the gut can send and receive impulses, record experience, and respond to emotions. In other words, the gut functioned very much like a brain.

We can use the gut as a brain and allow the head brain to rest. Why is this important? Because the head brain is a "monkey mind," riddled with doubt, shame, guilt, and suspicion. It is always thinking, planning, or worrying. Most people just think and think and think. Scientists have discovered that when people spend a lot of time worrying, their upper, head brain uses a lot of energy. They say that the upper brain can use up to 80 percent of the body's energy, leaving only 20 percent for the organs.

We need to use the brain in the head in order to perform complex functions such as reasoning, making plans, and making calculations. These are typical left-brain functions. However, for our daily life of consciousness, awareness, and feeling, which is typically governed by the right brain, we can use either the brain in the head or the brain in the gut. We should train the upper mind to be relaxed and to just observe when we do not need to be involved in specific mental activity. When we use the upper brain less, it becomes charged with energy and its power increases, and as a result more power is available to the body. When the upper brain is resting, brain repair and maintenance occur, and new brain cells can grow. This is the reason Taoism insists that we train the feeling and awareness brain in the gut—the "second brain"—so that we can use it when the upper brain is resting. With more charging of the upper brain, we have more power for creativity or whatever we want to use it for.

When you are not using the upper brain, allow it to rest by sending consciousness down to the lower Tan Tien, and send a warm, relaxed inner smile down to the abdominal area. Maintaining an awareness of the relaxed, smiling sensation in the lower Tan Tien is the first step in training the second brain. The key is to "seek the released mind" by relaxing, emptying, and sinking the upper mind down into the lower mind. We will discuss this further in Chapter 3.

SMILE DOWN TO THE LOWER BRAIN

Remember these guidelines:

1. Empty your mind down to the lower Tan Tien, and fill the lower Tan Tien with Chi. Move your conscious awareness from the head to the navel area—where the mind goes, the Chi flows—and allow your mind to direct all functions from the Tan Tien. See your "self" centered in the Tan Tien.

2. When your mind is empty, it will be filled. When the organs have extra energy, that extra energy will rise up and fill the brain with Chi.

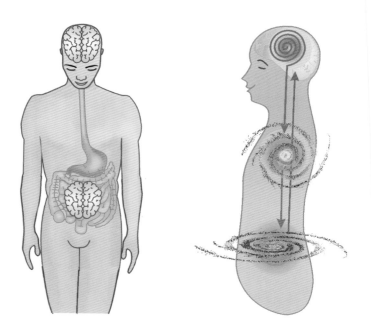

LEFT: LOWER TAN TIEN AND SECOND BRAIN CONNECTIONS
RIGHT: UPPER, MIDDLE, AND LOWER TAN TIEN CONNECTIONS

CHI AND TRANSFORMATION

In the Taoist vision, there are three kinds of bodies: the physical body, the energy body, and the spiritual or light body. The immaterial spiritual (high) body has its genesis in the transformation of the material physical (low) body. These two bodies are mutually dependent on each other and are connected with each other through the energy (soul) body.

The practice of Chi Kung involves all three bodies. If we practice only with the movements of the physical body, then we are merely performing physical exercise and are not truly practicing Chi Kung, for there is no training of energy. For effective control of energy, we have to enter the "Chi Kung state of mind." This is a meditative state that can also be called "entering silence." In the Chi Kung state, we can tap energy from the cosmos.

Through training in Tan Tien Chi Kung, the inner movements of body and mind become more natural. The Chi flow, generated by the Chi pressure in the lower Tan Tien, also becomes more natural, and will ultimately move by itself. As the Chi Kung state is cultivated, there will be a transition from an external to an internal direction of the movement of Chi, so that ultimately, the body moves by itself, carried forward by the invisible powers of the universe. One cultivates the "Wu Wei state," a state of actionless action, where it seems that nothing is done while in fact everything happens. Emptiness has generated fullness and nothing has produced everything.

As an inner energy practice, Tan Tien Chi Kung provides a focal point for a whole range of practices of the Universal Tao that promote various processes of transformation.

Chi Kung may be viewed as the practice by which separation and fragmentation, to which we are subject in our daily life as we become stressed and alienated from our true being, is overcome. We become inwardly united by the Chi flow as we are structurally properly aligned. In and through the practice, we learn to heal ourselves and become whole and undivided again, regaining our original state of being.

In the Taoist perspective, the recreation of unity within ourselves and the process of overcoming inner dispersion and fragmentation are crucial. This process is dependent on reestablishing within ourselves, through the practice, a sense of inner unity in which polarities are harmonized and one begins to feel at peace with oneself and the universe.

It is essential to this process that stagnations in the free flow of energy are overcome and the natural spontaneity of the movement of energy within the body and mind are restored. The practice serves to facilitate, enhance, and accommodate natural processes. The use of force ("pushing the river") has a contrary effect, as it tends to block the energy flow by creating tension in the body.

Tan Tien Chi Kung has a key role in setting in motion and sustaining these transformative processes, not only in terms of physical health and self-healing, but also for the purpose of mental balance and spiritual growth.

In Taoist tradition and in Chinese medicine, the physical body and its activities are viewed as yang, the energy body or Chi body is considered yin, and the spiritual body is the unity and marriage of the two. This explains the unique emphasis in Chi Kung on Chi and the subtle, inner structure of the energetic process in human development. Chi provides the link between the physical and the spiritual bodies and activates their processes of mutual support and transformation. For this reason, Chi has been likened to the fuel that feeds the engines of a boat. If there is little fuel and it is of poor quality, the ship is not likely to carry the passengers very far and the journey will end before they reach the other shore.

The process of transformation of the physical body into an energy body is generated by the mind, which guides and leads the Chi. The Chi will go where the mind leads it. As a consequence, the process of transformation is decisively dependent on the quality of mindfulness and awareness.

The process of awakening the body and its potential for self-transformation depends on the commitment to self-transformation. This takes form in the discipline one develops and the resulting focus and attention to the process. This discipline is not primarily an outer discipline and does not depend on any outer authority; it is an inner discipline, nourished by one's truthfulness with one's experience as the basis of practice. This then serves to awaken and remind one of one's inner commitment.

At the heart of Taoist practice stands the process of the alchemical conversion of energy: matter turns into energy and energy into matter of another kind and in another form. I have often observed that what is material dematerializes and what has dematerialized once again materializes into another form and state. Thus, the potential of the physical body to become a spiritual body is actualized.

As a rule, because of the materialistic perspective in today's dominant culture and the immediate utility of Chi Kung for enhancing health, some may tend to use it as another outer fitness practice. However, only those who make use of it its original intention develop inner power.

Unlimited Potentialities

OUR BODIES AND THE BODY OF THE UNIVERSE

The physical body cannot be seen as independent from the body of the universe, as if one could breathe and live without it or in spite of it. Intrinsic in the Taoist vision is the perception of one's own individual body as an expression of the loving body of the universe by which it was given birth, as is stated in the *Tao Te Ching*. By transcending the separation between oneself and the universe and honoring one's intrinsic unity with it, the universe becomes one's own body.

The Chi of the universe can only be absorbed to the extent that we open our heart to the universe and extend our consciousness and Chi to it as a token of our love. Only then will it respond. We will only receive the love energy of the universe to the extent that we acknowledge and honor our love relationship to it.

This first of all implies that we acknowledge that the universe is alive and that we are its children. Unless we awaken to this and bring it into our lives, it will be difficult to realize that we are part of it. We will tend to see ourselves as the center of the universe and to relate to the universe and the earth as objects to be conquered and manipulated. However, with increased sensitivity to our interconnectedness with the universe, a sense of responsibility, love, and compassion for the universe and the world will grow.

This experience of interconnectedness, rooted in the cultivation of love and compassion, is summarized in the ancient saying, "Embrace the universe as a mother her newborn child." Through the practice of Chi Kung, as we become grounded and connected and begin to feel at ease and relaxed in our body, this sense of unity is cultivated and reinforced.

When we relate with love and compassion to the universe, it will respond, and we will begin to feel it in the changes in the energy in our body. This is the law of reciprocity underlying our relationship with the universe.

In the practice of Chi Kung, of which Tan Tien Chi Kung is a particular form, a sudden sense of wonder may arise in a flash of awareness: although one is responsible for one's own life and for one's own breath and Chi, one realizes that one's breathing only exists because the universe breathes. This awareness then grows with the deep realization that one is part of the great whole and its rhythms; our awareness processes the life-giving energy. Such a sense of wonder may arise in between the out-breath and in-breath, and between the in-breath and out-breath, because these are moments of emptiness, when life is for a fraction in suspense.

However, in order to truly get in touch with the universe and with the world, we need to first love, be in touch with, and be connected with ourselves. In order to receive love, we need to give it so that a balance of reciprocity is maintained and enhanced on the basis of mutual exchange. And to be able to give, one must first gather abundant good energies to share. Sensitivity and a loving attitude toward oneself is thus a condition for getting in touch with others and with the energies of the universe.

Our relationship with the universe may be compared with that between two lovers. In order to attract the attention of the person with whom one has fallen in love, one needs to first share one's good intentions and qualities in order to stir openness and love on the other side. A true relationship is only possible if there is dialogue and partnership, a process of mutual exchange, and interplay of give and take.

THE CHI KUNG STATE AND
THE SENSE OF WONDER

Chi Kung is not a practice that is limited to strictly personal affairs. Rather, Chi Kung is a way of life and a state of being in which an inner practice cultivates positive and harmonious virtues and attitudes toward the universe and the community at large. This cultivation brings about in oneself the Chi Kung state of being, which can be understood as heightened state in which one is calm, clear, aware, strong, centered, and fully alive. This Chi Kung state of being nourishes and sustains harmonious forms of conduct in relation with the universe, nature, oneself, partners, family, neighbors, and people at large. Additionally, in the Chi Kung state, the processes of healing occur by themselves, as Chi is absorbed and directed naturally and spontaneously. Chi flows fluidly in the body, improving its physiological functions automatically as a variety of spontaneous adjustments take place.

Essential to spiritual growth in Taoist practice is the cultivation of a sense of purity, joyfulness, and wonder, thereby regaining and enhancing the openness and excitement of a small child. Not surprisingly, in the Taoist tradition the child represents purity and immortality.

In the *Tao Te Ching* Lao Tzu speaks of the wonders the higher cultivation of spirit energy may generate: from subtle wonders to mysterious wonders to incredible wonders. These are not to be understood as romantic metaphors but actual processes of Chi transformation by Chi Kung masters. Taoist masters cultivate the ability to be moved by and to move high energy frequencies, in ways that are inexplicable by orthodox materialist science.

We can sense the potential for this state in and around ourselves, for underneath conventional awareness there is another, wholly different form of awareness. In this state what is conventionally conceived as impossible is precisely that which inspires us in our Chi Kung practice.

This state of wonder and possibility has been characteristic of all the great Taoist, Buddhist, Hindu, and other great masters throughout history. They defied, by their inner sense of freedom, the rules as well as the perceptions of the society in which they lived. The high degree of spontaneity, humor, and joyfulness exhibited by these individuals was sometimes called "crazy fellowship" as it was so uncommon and often broke with the society's standards.

As we practice Chi Kung, we may recognize our "old state of being" as the outcome of a process of conditioning by our cultures in which we close down to our innate potentialities. We may realize that we have been taught to believe that extraordinary virtues and capacities were only the privilege of highly endowed people, unlike ourselves, in the distant past.

Yet, unlimited innate capacities move within our own innermost being, the "unconscious" state deep within ourselves. As we practice, we get in touch with the hidden liberative potential within ourselves, beneath the crust of our active functional consciousness, and come to sense the power of the invisible creative energy that awaits our invitation to be actualized.

HIGHER CULTIVATION

In modern Western culture, as a result of a long historical process, there has been a progressive disconnection between body and mind, and a subordination and repression of body, sensation, emotions, instinct, and nature. Consciousness was reduced to what was in accordance with the demands for rationality, self-control, outer discipline, and other requirements of modern industrial society. The unconscious and subconscious were viewed as states that interfered with these values.

In Taoist practice, deep relaxation and inner peace or stillness enable us to suspend our ordinary consciousness and get in touch with the deep unconscious or subconscious state. In this way, we can sense what our body tells us, what signals it wants to transmit.

Sensitivity to the consciousness in our glands, energy pathways, blood, lymph system, bones, joints, heart, and all the other organs and parts of our body is an expression of the Chi Kung state. We cannot always live in this state, but once we have access to it and know how it feels to be connected with the source of our primordial life experience, we can easily return to it.

In the Chi Kung state we get in touch with our reservoirs of latent inner energies and transform our Jing (generative energy/sexual essence) into Chi, and Chi into Shen (spiritual energy). New states cannot arrive without old states transforming; the new grows out of the old.

Historically, withdrawal from the world has always been associated with meditative practice. Yet meditation can also serve to make us better able to live *in* the world. We are in touch with our true self, centered and grounded in our lower Tan Tien. We are not too much affected by the storms of life because we are able to move into our center, where stillness reigns. Tan Tien Chi Kung is a precious practice that creates a state of energetic self-reliance and allows us to get in touch with our hidden reservoir of high frequencies and energies.

ENERGY TRANSFORMATION AND THE LOWER TAN TIEN

The lower Tan Tien contains the basic spark that was created when your father's sperm penetrated your mother's egg. If this spark continues to be active and strong, it provides life force to the billions of cells throughout your body. Control of sexual energy and its transformation into life force is essential if we wish to raise our energy level in the lower Tan Tien. For men this implies preserving the life essence of the sperm during intercourse or self-stimulation. Through controlling ejaculation they can transform the sexual essence/generative energy (Jing) of the sperm into Chi. For women it means learning to regulate and control menstruation, thereby transforming the generative essence in the blood into Chi. The practices for cultivating the ability to control and transform sexual energy are presented in the first two chapters of *Taoist Cosmic Healing* by Mantak Chia. In the Universal Tao System, it is very important to learn how to transform sexual energy into spiritual energy. The original balance between love and sex, or water and fire, contains in itself the essence of healing and creation. Another vital transformation that occurs within the lower Tan Tien is the transformation of negative emotions. (A thorough explanation of these processes may be found in the books *Healing Love* and *Cultivating Male or Female Sexual Energy* by Mantak Chia.)

As a functional practice, the focus in Chi Kung is on its immediate effects. For example, in the Healing Love practice, life energy is saved, health is enhanced, and the organs are regenerated. Chi Kung is at the same time, however, a practice by which Chi is transformed into spirit, and lower-energy substances are transformed into higher-energy substances. Once the energy in the lower Tan Tien has become pure and strong through the transformation of sexual energy and negative emotions, it will then naturally ascend to the middle and upper Tan Tiens and be transformed into Shen, or spiritual energy. At every stage, as one comes closer to unity with the Tao, the energies take on a more refined and subtle form.

In the Healing Love practice, it is not that a sacred body is created out of a profane body. The body was always sacred. However, through the practice, awareness is cultivated through which our experience undergoes a revolution: we deeply realize and experience in a new way the fact that the material body and the material universe are made of the same indivisible substance. We become aware of what is already present—the profound sacredness of our own body. Once this realization has taken hold, our bodies begin to react and grow in a positive manner.

In this way, we learn to create a sacred and holy temple within ourselves, and we begin to integrate our physical, mental, and spirit bodies. Cultivation and transformation of sexual energy is an important part of this integration. We become more aware of all aspects of the self, and the separation between the different parts of ourselves is bridged and a synergy is created.

The Taoist practice provides us with the resources to extend beyond the realm of our senses. By tapping into our internal resources and channeling the energy around us, we can perceive much more than the senses normally report to the mind. The energy that one cultivates and experiences may reach levels and forms that are wholly beyond the imagination of the conventional mind as it is molded by cultural conditioning that severely restricts our sense of human potential.

Smiling and Laughing Chi Kung

BODY SENSING

In Chi Kung practice, the art of sensing and feeling is the primary form of cognition, taking precedence over all other forms of knowledge. Our mind directs and guides Chi, but if we cannot feel and sense our body, the mind cannot give direction and guidance. To be able to feel and sense, our nervous system needs to be in a relaxed state. The moment we are stressed and tense, our ability to feel and sense the processes in our body declines. We tend to then become even more disconnected from our body, and as a result, become more confused and upset.

As members of industrial and postindustrial cultures, we have to relearn to value and listen to our body and become sensitive to what it wants to tell us. Modern life has increasingly emphasized abstract cognition over other forms of knowledge, particularly embodied forms of knowledge. Widespread "dis-ease" is a result of the sharp decline of basic body awareness and a generalized lowering of Chi pressure. This feeling of "dis-ease" generates negative emotions that are then projected onto people and the world around us. Precisely because of the desperate conditions this situation engenders and the resistance it creates, there is an awakening to the need for a new, more embodied way of understanding ourselves and the universe.

Tan Tien Chi Kung is a very effective practice in the process of relearning to be open to the many dimensions of ourselves and to connect with our own body. And as we become more centered in and aware of our bodies, we can more easily be open to others and to the world around us.

THE INNER SMILE

The Inner Smile is a powerful relaxation and self-healing technique that uses the energy of love, happiness, kindness, and gentleness as a

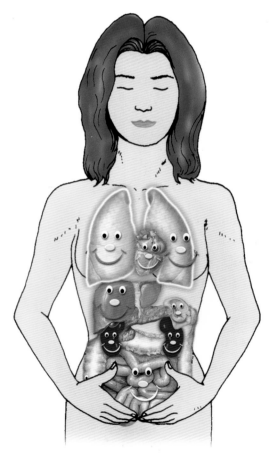

INNER SMILE

language to communicate with the internal organs of the body. The practice also aids the transformation of negative emotions into positive, virtuous energy. This transformation is a very powerful Chi Kung practice. A genuine smile transforms negative energy into loving energy that has the power to relax, balance, and heal. By learning to smile inwardly to the organs and glands, you will cause your whole body to feel loved and appreciated and to enjoy more Chi.

The process of internal transformation in Tan Tien Chi Kung starts with the Inner Smile practice, in which we send a warm, loving Inner Smile down to the lower brain and lower abdominal area. It is the key practice for keeping Chi pressure in the lower Tan Tien and the whole body, and is the most effective practice for keeping all energy routes in the body open.

Although the Inner Smile at first sight would appear to be an easy practice, it actually represents a great challenge. It holds in all its apparent simplicity a highly concentrated way to change our whole attitude toward life and toward ourselves. It is the key to shifting and transforming our inner disposition and attitude so that we open ourselves to the ability to "flow with the stream of life." It helps us learn to not "push against the river" and use force on ourselves and others. It trains us to accept ourselves and others so that, as we raise our awareness and mindfulness, transformation can come from within and not from above or outside.

The practice of the Inner Smile is not a shrewd trick or an easy device to forget or repress our pain. We need to recognize that we will invariably experience existential and other forms of pain as a natural part of the ups and downs of life. What the Inner Smile practice does is train us to look deeply into ourselves and to transform the pain into a source of self-transformation and empowerment. We become truly invulnerable not by ignoring pain but by becoming more vulnerable and in touch with ourselves. By so doing, we can be more sensitive to others and to the world. It is good to shed tears as we detoxify ourselves. In a patriarchal culture like ours, men are not supposed to shed tears because it shows their weakness. As we learn the Inner Smile, we open up to our deeper self and learn to process our pain. In this way we restore the energy flow so that we can laugh and smile again as we learn to embrace ourselves, others, and the world. The Inner Smile practice trains us to sense, feel, see, and hear deeply; it trains us to accept and embrace what is there so that our experience of life is opened up again.

By smiling into our whole body and being, we affirm the intrinsic goodness of existence and our gratitude for being alive. The inner smile creates the ground for self-esteem, which is necessary to develop inner dignity and self-empowerment.

The Inner Smile may be seen as a first process of alchemical transformation on which all the others depend; it is the beginning of a new way of being. The practice teaches us to accept ourselves as we are, with a unique blend of good and negative energies. We need both of them in order to grow. Without the negative energies there would be no impulse for the transformation process and we could not raise our energy supply. The energy potential hidden in negative energies would remain repressed and untapped.

SMILING AND LAUGHING
ENERGY PRACTICES

Smiling and lowering the upper mind down to the lower mind, the lower Tan Tien, is of particular importance as a way to tune in to our life source and raise our life force. By so doing, we make it possible for the diaphragm to relax and freely move up and down. This also makes the lungs and heart happy. Laughing and smiling are perhaps the best ways to connect with the lower Tan Tien, generate Chi pressure and inner power, restore the free flow of energy, and increase immunity.

It is good to experiment with and experience different forms of smiling and laughing. We then learn to bring our smiling and laughing within us, shifting from outward smiling and laughing to inner smiling and laughing. It is a process like hitting a drum on its outside

OUTWARD LAUGHING

and causing vibrations inside; the vibrations start on the outside but resonate within. With inner laughing, the vibrations are more subtle in the lower Tan Tien, and more powerful Chi pressure is generated. The more inward the smile is, the less the lungs are used and the more energy is economized and natural (embryonic) breathing is approached.

Smiling and laughing Chi Kung are such natural forms of relaxation that we hardly think of them as a Chi Kung practice. Yet they are among the most effective ways to restore the water energy/fire energy balance in the body. By making the sound *"Ha,"* as we do while laughing, heat is released and excess fire energy is expelled, and the body is cooled and thereby rebalanced. The sound *"Ha"* together with the sounds *"Ho"* and *"Hum"* constitute a triad of sounds that serve as seed mantras in the hundred-syllable mantra in Tibetan Buddhist practice, by which the highest wisdom energies are invoked. The very low sounds that Tibetan monks make when chanting their mantras are very similar to those heard on NASA recordings from space of the sounds of Earth, Saturn, and other planets. The deep mantra tones originate from deep in the belly and thereby

INNER LAUGHING

create powerful vibrations in the lower Tan Tien, raising internal
pressure and power to move Chi.

Specific sounds raise particular energy frequencies in each organ.
The sound *"Ha"* is the sound that makes the whole body feel good, as
it generates Chi and makes energies move, so that a state of well-
being is experienced.

The Inner Smile is not only essential to get in touch with ourselves. It is also the key that makes it possible for us to get in touch
with, receive, and absorb universal, earth, and cosmic energies.

Smiling down into the body has multiple beneficial effects,
including releasing toxins, restoring the energy flow, and increasing
the capacity of the body to heal itself.

The Inner Smile begins at the eyes and the mid-eyebrow point
and moves down to the heart and then to the lower Tan Tien. As you

GROUP LAUGHING

activate the heart, loving energy will flow out and you will feel the energy of your Inner Smile flow down the entire length of your body like a waterfall. This is a very powerful and effective tool to counteract stress, tension, and negative Chi.

As we physically relax, letting go of muscular and emotional tensions, and turn on our very special subtle smile, we gain access to the inner realms. We open the pathways of the parasympathetic nervous system and become more alert in inner sensing.

Inner Smile energy practice #1

1. This exercise teaches us to smile to the mid-eyebrow, eyebrows, eyes, mouth, jaw, tongue, lips, cheeks, ears, shoulders, rib cage, and brain. We then let the observing mind (the upper brain) sink down into the lower Tan Tien. Practice this exercise until you become familiar and comfortable with it. Begin by smiling to the mid-eyebrow. Relax and let go of all mental, emotional,

INNER SMILE SPIRALING OUT TO THE UNIVERSE

and physical tension. Smile to the eyebrows, and visualize them growing long to the sides.

2. Smile to the eyes. Relax the eyes and feel how nice and cool they are. Let the eyes draw back in their sockets and start to sink down to the chest and gradually down to the abdomen, the home of your feeling and awareness mind.

3. Relax the two broad muscles extending from the outer portions of the upper lips across the cheekbones. Lightly smile, feeling the muscles' connection to the upper front of the ears. Gradually feel the ears growing long (up and down).

4. Open your mouth and relax your jaw, separating the upper and lower teeth. Feel the jaw relax. Once the jaw relaxes, the shoulders will relax and drop down. Continue to feel the jaw relax until you feel saliva start to come out. Relax down to the rib cage. Feel the rib cage drop down, softening all the joints, relaxing down to the lower Tan Tien. Let the tongue relax back in

the mouth. Feel the tongue start to drop down into the throat. Visualize all the energies of the head and face sinking down into the chest and all the way down to the navel and lower Tan Tien.

5. Smile to the shoulders. Relax until you feel the shoulders drop and the rib cage relax.

6. Lightly close the lips, but keep the teeth slightly separated. Physically begin a childlike smile, with the corners of the mouth gently uplifted and the outer edges of the eyes softly crinkled up. Breathe through your nose.

7. Smile into the brain and continue to empty the upper (observing) mind into the lower Tan Tien.

8. Become aware of your inner universe as vast, empty space. Keep on sinking down, into the darkness of your empty space. Keep sinking, and experience the vastness. Stay relaxed and alert. Rest.

Inner Smile energy practice #2

1. First laughter: start either standing or sitting with both palms covering the navel—left hand over right for men, right hand over left for women. Start to laugh out loud and feel the abdominal vibration. Laugh out loud continuously for five minutes. Rest, cover the navel with the palms, and feel it become warm. Visualize a warm, bright ball of energy in your abdomen. Then visualize the ball of energy forming a spiral (the Tai Chi or yin/yang spiral). Visualize the energy spiraling in a clockwise direction. Then visualize the energy spiraling in a counterclockwise direction.

2. Second laughter: begin practicing inner laughing, which is like a tickling in the throat. Continue to feel the warm ball of energy in the navel, and continue to visualize this ball of energy spiraling clockwise, and then counterclockwise. This will keep the Chi in the navel area.

3. Third laughter: begin practicing the silent, inner laughter, which is like the vibration that resonates on the inside of a

drum. Keep the vibration resonating inside you for five minutes. Rest, keeping the navel covered with your palms. Spiral the energy in the navel, as described above, to store the energy in this area.

Inner Smile energy practice #3

1. Focusing your awareness on the mid-eyebrow, close your eyes and imagine that you are in one of your favorite places in the world, a place where you feel safe, relaxed, and happy. Recall the sights you saw there, the sounds you heard, and the scents, sensations, and flavors you associate with that place.

2. Imagine that one of your favorite people is standing in front of you, smiling to you with loving, happy, radiant, shining eyes. Smile to your own face, slightly lifting up the corners of your mouth.

3. Feel yourself responding to that special person's smile with a smile of your own. Feel your eyes smiling and relaxing.

4. Smile down to the thymus gland and picture a white flower blossoming. Gently inhale into the thymus gland, connecting your breath to the olfactory organ. Smell the good fragrance.

5. Aim your inner attention at your heart. Picture the heart before your inner eye and smile to it. Smile until you feel the heart smile back to you. Picture your heart like a red rose, gradually opening. This will activate the love and fire of compassion in the heart. The heart's red light and loving awareness will, in turn, activate the cosmic red healing light or mist from above and around you.

6. Smile at the red light or mist and very slowly, with a soft, long, deep breath, draw the red mist, love, and compassion into the mid-eyebrow, down through the mouth and throat, and into the heart, where it gradually overflows to the small intestine. Retaining the red light and the love and compassion in the heart and small intestine, exhale the cloudy black or negative energy. Repeat this breathing eighteen to thirty-six times, or until the

heart becomes bright red before your inner vision and starts to radiate loving red light out to the tongue, mouth, nose, ears, and eyes. Allow the red light to whirl around you and form a red aura. Feel your skin glowing with red energy.

7. Let the heart's loving energy radiate out to the lungs. Aim your attention at the lungs; picture them before your inner eye and smile to them. Smile until you feel the lungs smile back to you. Picture your lungs like a white rose, gradually opening; smell the good fragrance. This will activate the courage in the lungs. Once you invoke the white light and courage to shine from within the lungs, you will also activate the cosmic white healing light or mist from above and around you.

8. Smile at the white light or mist and very slowly, with a soft, long, deep breath, draw the white mist into the mid-eyebrow, down through the mouth and throat, and into the lungs, where it gradually overflows into the large intestine. Retaining the white light and the feeling of courage in the lungs, exhale the cloudy black or negative energy. Repeat this breathing eighteen to thirty-six times, or until the lungs become bright white and start to radiate the white light of courage out to the nose, ears, eyes, tongue, and mouth. Invite the white light to whirl around you and form a white aura covering your skin like autumn dew.

9. The spleen, pancreas, and stomach correspond to the yellow color of the earth element. Aim your attention at these organs; picture them before your inner eye, and smile to them. Smile until you feel them smile back to you. First connect to the heart. The heart is the root of compassion, and it is always a good idea to take a moment and connect with the heart and feel its connection to the other organs. Picture the spleen center as a yellow rose, slowly opening and radiating a yellow light. This will activate the cosmic yellow healing light or mist from above and around you. You might see the golden yellow aura of a wheat field ready for harvest.

10. Smile at the yellow light or mist and very slowly, with a soft, long, deep breath, draw it into the mid-eyebrow, down through the mouth and throat, and into the spleen center. Fill the spleen center with the golden yellow light. Exhaling, expel feelings of worry and the cloudy, sticky energy. Repeat this breathing eighteen to thirty-six times. Then allow the light to radiate out to your mouth, nose, ears, eyes, and tongue. Wrap the golden aura around you, leaving a golden shine on your skin.

11. The kidneys and bladder correspond to the blue color of the water element. Aim your attention at these organs; picture them before your inner eye, and smile to them. Smile until you feel them smiling back to you. Picture the kidneys as a blue rose, slowly opening. See them radiate the blue healing light of gentleness. Once you've invoked the blue light of the kidneys, you will also activate the blue cosmic light above and around you.

12. Smile at the blue light or mist around you and very slowly, with a soft, long, deep breath, draw it into the mid-eyebrow, down through the mouth and throat, and into the kidneys. Retaining the blue light and the feeling of gentleness, exhale, expelling feelings of fear or stress and the cloudy or negative energy. Repeat eighteen to thirty-six times, or until the blue light of gentleness starts to radiate out from your kidneys to your ears, eyes, tongue, mouth, and nose. Gather the blue mist on your skin, enveloping yourself in a blue aura.

13. The liver and gallbladder correspond to the green color of the element wood. Focus your attention on these organs; picture them before your inner eye and smile to them. Smile until you feel them smile back at you. Picture them as a green rose, slowly opening and radiating green healing light of kindness. Once you've invoked the green light of the liver and gallbladder, you will also activate the green cosmic light above and around you.

14. Smile at the green light or mist around you and very slowly, with a soft, long, deep breath, draw it into the mid-eyebrow,

down through the mouth and throat, and into the liver and gall-bladder. Retaining the green light and the feeling of kindness, exhale, expelling the dark red cloudy heat of anger. Inhale the nourishing green of the forests, inviting in kindness. Repeat eighteen to thirty-six times, or until the green light has completely filled the liver and starts to radiate out to your eyes, tongue, mouth, nose, and ears. Invite the green light to form a green aura around you.

15. Smile down to the sexual organs and reproductive system. Smile until you feel them smile back to you. Feel the heart (love) and sexual organs (arousal) uniting. Observe how this process transforms sexual energy into Chi. Now imagine this Chi as a beautiful, gentle pink color that radiates from your sexual organs. Thank the sexual organs for their work in keeping you alive and healthy.

16. Rest. Do nothing. Gather and store the energy by smiling and use your mind to "spiral" the energy to the lower Tan Tien. (Spiraling is a way to condense Chi in an area so that it may be stored.)

Inner Smile energy practice #4

1. Sit, stand, or lay down in a comfortable position.
2. Cover the navel with the palms—left hand over right for men, right hand over left for women.
3. Smile into the mid-eyebrow and feel it relax. Smile and relax the upper mind, and allow it to sink, moving slowing down to the neck, down to the chest, and gradually down to the lower Tan Tien.
4. Feel the navel area starting to get warm. Visualize a ball of energy in this area, and then visualize this energy spiraling like the Tai Chi (yin/yang) spiral. Feel the Chi getting warmer and warmer.
5. Feel the Chi in the navel area getting warmer and warmer and starting to rise up through the spine to the brain.

6. Keep five percent of your awareness on the spiral of energy in your lower abdomen. At the same time, visualize the energy that has risen up to the brain begin to form a spiral in the head. Continue to spiral that energy, feeling the Chi pressure in the brain begin to grow.

7. Feel the Chi pressure pushing outward as it grows stronger. Gradually guide the Chi into the sinuses and allow it to build until you feel the Chi pressure push down into the nose and open the sinuses. Feel the nose open and your breathing improved. Moving Chi down into the sinuses in this way may help prevent colds and flu.

8. Touch your tongue to the roof of your mouth. In this way, you will link the Governor Channel (the line of energy that runs up the spine) to the Functional Channel (the line of energy that runs down the front of the torso), thus connecting the Microcosmic Orbit. Slowly let the Chi drop down by itself to the navel area. Smile down into the navel a while and feel the energy being condensed and safely stored in the lower Tan Tien. Remember to always bring the energy back to the lower Tan Tien, as this is the best place to store it. It is unsafe to leave excess Chi in your organs, as this may cause the organs to accumulate too much energy and overheat from the process.

Squatting Chi Kung

A NATURAL POSTURE

One of the most wonderful Tan Tien Chi Kung exercises undoubtedly is squatting. It is a very common posture in many regions of the world that have been less affected by modernization. In these regions squatting is considered a relaxing posture, yet in the modern West it is now considered "exercise."

Since the beginning of civilization, people have known the highly beneficial effects of squatting. Their bodies told them to do so and in this way they created a deep state of relaxation in which the sacrum and spine are open and the warm life current in the body maintains an optimal, free flow.

Squatting is also closely connected with togetherness. When people in traditional communities relax, they often squat together in a circle. It is also the ideal position for work in the fields, as work can be easily alternated with moments of rest. It is also part of the realm of play and playfulness among children.

As the squatting position generates a state of relaxation and stillness, it is also a natural posture for meditative practice. In many indigenous cultures, people assume the squatting position precisely for that reason.

It is not incidental that this yoga position (in the original meaning of the Sanskrit word *yoga*, which means "union") is the one that

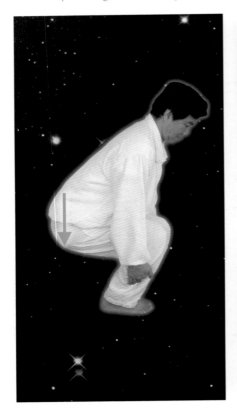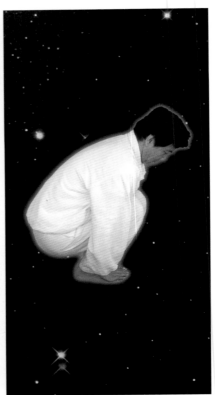

SQUATTING POSITION

comes closest to that of the child in its embryonic high-energy state. In the squatting posture, our capacity for energy storage is optimal, the metabolic rate is low, and energy consumption most economical.

The sleeping posture in which one lies on one's side with the legs pulled in is similar to the squatting position. The subconscious counsels this position for its regenerating quality.

In many cultures, when people die they are laid in the squatting position because it resembles most closely that of the child before it was born. Thus body is thus laid to rest in a position that reconnects the body with its original state of being.

Squatting may perhaps be called Tan Tien Chi Kung exercise number one, but let's protect its entirely natural character for those

SQUATTING TO CONNECT WITH MOTHER EARTH AND THE GALAXY BELOW

who are spontaneous Chi Kung practitioners without knowing it. Our body naturally knows the wisdom of this posture.

SQUATTING AND THE PSOAS

More than any other posture, squatting opens the lower lumbar vertebrae and thereby prevents hernia. It also activates the latent motor force of the pelvis, opens the groin, flexes the hip joints, induces downward pressure and release of waste, gases, and toxins, and reactivates the colon. (Squatting has been the position humans historically have used to move the bowels.) By the gravity pull it provokes, it stirs the earth Chi current to move and bounce upward to the perineum, awakening the spinal fluids in the sacrum, and opening and elongating the spine. This action rebalances the vertebrae and eases the Chi current upward to the crown.

Additionally, the squatting posture massages the lungs and heart. The lower Tan Tien helps the heart by facilitating and activating the Chi and blood flow.

Of particular importance is the role of squatting in lengthening the psoas, the muscles in the groin area that rotate the hip joint and flex the spine. The psoas tend to shorten with age, and can also be affected by anxiety and oversensitivity to cold temperatures. Shortening of the psoas pulls the body out of alignment and interferes with the correct upward and downward flow of Chi.

Maintaining suppleness in the psoas muscles is so important that there are Tao Yin practices that focus particularly on this area. The psoas is called the "soul muscle" in Chinese. In order for the soul to develop and for its eventual transference upward through the crown,

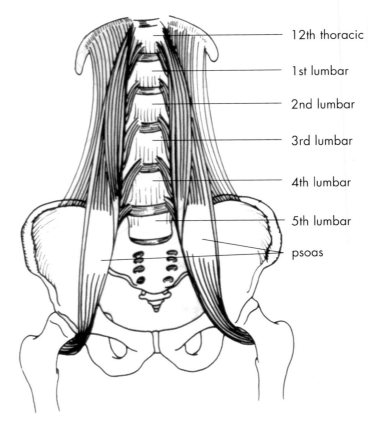

- 12th thoracic
- 1st lumbar
- 2nd lumbar
- 3rd lumbar
- 4th lumbar
- 5th lumbar
- psoas

RELAXED PSOAS CONTRIBUTE TO OPTIMUM CHI FLOW

it needs a well-aligned, straight body, in line with earth and heaven.

By relaxing the psoas, unity between the lower and the upper parts of the body is promoted. A flexible psoas makes it possible for the Chi to freely flow upward, connecting the lower lumbar with the lower part of the groin. When the psoas muscles are relaxed, the earth Chi can freely flow from the legs into the spine and upper body (via the perineum and sacrum).

Supple psoas muscles also facilitate free Chi flow between the kidneys and the heart. The free exchange between the fire Chi from the heart and the water Chi from the kidneys enables the kidneys to be warmed and the heart cooled. This is the basis of the balance between water and fire energy in the whole body, and thereby the balance between yin and yang.

SQUATTING PRACTICES

It is recommending that one practice squatting for three to five minutes each day to maintain good health and flexibility.

Squatting using a wall

1. A good exercise for developing the squatting posture is to stand with your feet shoulder width apart, close to a wall (eighteen centimeters or more away from the wall), facing the wall. As you improve your squatting ability, you can move closer to the wall, and place the feet closer together.

2. Place both hands on the sides, the tips of the fingers touching the sides of the thighs.

3. Slowly drop straight down from the groin area, like you are sitting down. The wall will prevent you from leaning forward too much when you squat. Some people tend to lean the head and neck forward and the buttocks back. Using a wall will help you to see whether you are bending forward too much.

4. Drop until you can't go any further, and lightly bend the knees.

5. Breathe into the lower Tan Tien. Keep the chest relaxed.

6. As you squat down to the earth, feel a force pulling you down and a counterforce pulling you up.

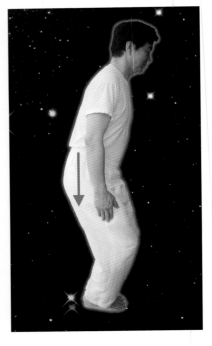

FACING A WALL, SQUAT STRAIGHT DOWN FROM THE GROIN

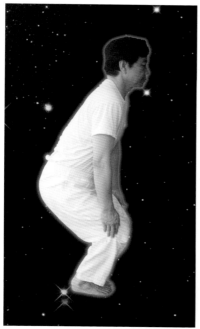

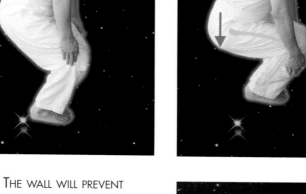

THE WALL WILL PREVENT
YOU FROM BENDING FORWARD
TOO MUCH

Squatting with a partner

1. You can also practice squatting with the help of a partner or the edge of a table. When you work with a partner, stand facing each other, two to three feet apart. Place your feet shoulder-width apart.

2. Stretch your arms toward your partner and firmly grasp one another's wrists.

3. From this position, squat straight down together from the groin while supporting one another.

4. Sink as deep as you both can without leaning forward.

5. Breathe into the lower Tan Tien. Keep the chest relaxed.

6. As you squat down to the earth, feel a force pulling you down and a counterforce pulling you up.

SQUAT WITH YOUR PARTNER, SUPPORTING ONE ANOTHER

Breathing, Dancing, and Bone Chi Kung

NATURAL BREATHING

Abdominal Breathing

The natural form of breathing is abdominal breathing. This is the principal measure by which to evaluate the body's state of health and capacity for self-healing. To the extent that we practice abdominal breathing, we have retained the natural way we used to breathe as a baby and child.

When, in the course of life, natural, low, deep, long, and quiet abdominal breathing is replaced by high, short, and shallow breathing in the chest, we lose our inner stability. We have lost a major source of vitality and self-healing, as our breathing requires more energy than it generates. We lose inner Chi pressure, and we lose the vital balance between the inner Chi pressure in the body and outer pressure from the atmosphere and environment.

We can only regain our vitality by recreating this internal power pressure so that the two pressures are once again in a dynamic and reciprocal state of interplay. Through the cultivation of deep, natural abdominal breathing, we recover our original Chi and thereby our internal Chi pressure. As we practice deep abdominal breathing, we build and maintain Chi pressure. Gradually, deep, abdominal breathing becomes very easy and automatic. The more natural it becomes, the more it enhances the free and full flow of original Chi throughout the whole body, its reservoirs, pathways, organs, glands, fascia, and all cells.

This kind of breathing may be compared to that in a deep and calm sleep. It is not without reason that when we see children sleeping, we are struck by the beauty and serenity of their expression and the peaceful energy they radiate. We feel the fine and good energies they emanate and it seems as if the inner quality of the Chi in the child's body becomes transparent.

Deep abdominal breathing does not rely exclusively on external oxygen and external Chi, as it also draws on original Chi. The abdomen starts to breathe by itself and the process of breathing becomes economical, effortless, and unintentional. Inner breath and outer breath have a relationship as the external breath can move the inner breath and vice versa. "External breath" refers to the physical act of breathing, regardless of which technique you use. "Internal breath" methods directly focus the mind within the physical body, awakening subtle body energies and conducting the Chi using pure awareness. Chi pressure from the lower Tan Tien helps the lungs to breathe deeply. The way the lungs are used also affects the internal breath. Genuine inner breathing can only evolve if external breathing gives it space. Lower abdominal breathing is an external breathing technique used to facilitate the internal breath.

Through deep abdominal breathing, the amount of energy needed for external breathing and the intake of oxygen are reduced. Precisely because of this, the lungs can then take in more oxygen. At the same time, the capacity of the whole body and all its cells as well as the capacity of the lungs to store oxygen is enhanced. Thus, with less energy, breathing improves both qualitatively and quantitatively.

Skin Breathing

In prenatal breathing, the body doesn't breathe through the nose, but through the whole body. This is at times called "skin breathing," although the whole body is involved. Skin breathing is a higher form of breathing that we gradually cultivate as we practice Chi Kung. In skin breathing, there is an automatic generation and direction of Chi and a spontaneous rejuvenation of the body.

In skin breathing, on the in-breath, Chi flows to the bone marrow and organs. Red and white blood cells are created and renewed in the bone marrow; these cells are needed to transport the supply of nutrition, to remove waste, and to neutralize germs. They then replenish the organs with fresh energy. On the out-breath, the Chi flows to the tendons, muscles, and skin, expelling waste through the pores of the skin and opening it for fresh Chi to enter.

Thus skin breathing regulates the continuous exchange process between inner and outer energies. Brushing one's skin with a soft brush enhances this natural exchange process. In the state of skin breathing, the borders between the inside and outside of the body tend to dissolve and a sense of unity with the universe may arise by itself. One feels at the same time at home within the body and in the universe, which is then experienced as one's own extended body.

Natural breathing—both abdominal breathing and skin breathing—become possible when emotional fixations and entanglements are overcome so that we feel at peace with ourselves, relaxed, calm, and happy. To induce this process, the practice of the Inner Smile is of crucial significance. It helps to clear the energy reservoirs and pathways and also enhances the state of receptivity of the bones, organs, glands, and cells so that the flow of Chi can enter and do its work.

INNER AND OUTER DANCING

Dancing and shaking the body is very beneficial for the lymph system and is very good for our bones and joints. Dancing is a way to rebalance ourselves and regenerate our joyfulness and good humor. As we dance, we experience joy. We firmly touch the earth, which responds by sending Chi upward into our bodies. When we let the bones dance, we fill the joints and the spaces in between with Chi.

The more "inward" our dance becomes, as a form of energy meditation, the deeper will be the effect. There is evidence that Chi Kung in its earliest stages was a form of slow dance in which healing qualities were realized. The Taoist dance form, with its slow, rhythmic, gentle, and graceful movements, is an expression of the inner movement of the life force. The highest form of dancing is one in which we inwardly balance the dynamic relations between the elements and phases in our body with our surroundings. We then enter into a state of equilibrium and so merge with the Tao.

The more bones dance from within and in unison with the universe, the more dancing becomes a healing practice. Chi from all directions flows in and out and harmonizes, each time creating the inner power and pressure needed to infuse Chi power and gentleness in the next movement. The secret of the power and elegance of the natural movement of animals is the natural equilibrium they maintain.

In indigenous cultures, dancing was seen as a sacred form of expression. It opens a space to experience the divine directly through the vibrations it generates and the unity of yin and yang it enhances. In such a form of dance, people are not only involved as individuals separate from each other, but they also experience their unity and connections with other as a community and with the universe. In this way a regenerative process is set in motion and the unity of the community with the universe is reaffirmed. There is a state of dynamic balance in which we feel connected with ourselves and with the whole.

The Taoist style of dance brings the center of gravity down to the lower Tan Tien so that we enhance the ability to move from our center. This enables the Chi pressure to build up and naturally move the body in natural waves.

Dancing has an intrinsic erotic and ecstatic quality, as it serves to transform the Jing, or generative energy/sexual essence, into Chi, and stimulate the hormone flow. Dancing may therefore be considered a particular form of Healing Love practice.

It is not by coincidence that the traditional dances of many ancient cultures continue today. Dancing is connected with marriage celebrations, and is also common to great mystical rituals, in which it becomes the ecstatic expression of unity with the divine.

Belly dancing is a form of ritual dance that is closely connected with rituals of fertility and invoking the feminine powers of the universe. By pressing the ground and swinging the hips, the groin opens, and as the Chi from the earth flows upward, the sexual organ and the whole pelvic floor are stimulated and the life force starts to fill the belly. It then begins to tremble and vibrate and the Chi moves to the sacrum, up the spine, and through the whole body, filling the reservoirs, energy routes, organs, and glands.

This form of ritual dance was originally done by women among themselves, as men were not allowed into the women's sacred, life-giving circle. It regenerates the life current and thereby grants a heightened sense of inner power, joyful vitality, and self-esteem. It is therefore not surprising that belly dancing has come back in circles of women who seek to raise their autonomy and self-esteem as well as their joyfulness in life.

Thus, dancing in which the mind, Chi, and body are properly aligned with heaven and earth may be seen as a particular form of Chi Kung. People practice Chi Kung as it helps them to generate, regain, and balance their life force and thereby enter into the Chi Kung state. They get more in touch with the energies of the universe and their own energy and inner power.

If we lead the flow of the Chi with our Yi (the Yi is a fusion of our upper, lower, and middle minds into one mind), the dance may turn into a kind of single-cultivation Healing Love practice, as we unite yin and yang within ourselves. Or, as men and women perform sacred dance together, they can practice another form of Healing Love practice, as mind, body, and breath mutually adjust in the dance.

Through practicing sacred forms of dance, in alignment with Taoist Chi Kung principles, a high quality of natural Chi pressure is built in both the body and the mind, and balance is restored within and without. When practiced in conjunction with forms of the Healing Love practice, through the cultivation of love, compassion, and other qualities of being, there is alignment with the forces of the universe. A whole new range of physical and spiritual transformations in our mind and body become possible.

Tai Chi masters often seem to move like tigers. This may have an "electrifying" effect on the surroundings and those who see and feel them, as Chi is emitted and the Chi in the empathetic onlooker starts to resonate. Although the tiger is fully grounded at each step and movement, they move very lightly. They are totally relaxed and calm, yet highly awake and alert. One feels highly concentrated power, which can be mobilized at any moment into any direction. One feels stillness in the movement and movement in the stillness.

In practitioners of sacred dance, one senses and sees the power of the mind and Chi combine in the power of the movement. That is also the reason why dance, as a practice to unite heaven and earth within yourself, has a transformational effect on the dancer as well as on those who see them and join in the dance.

True dancing only arises if and when the movement starts from the center, the lower Tan Tien. For this reason Tan Tien Chi Kung is an essential practice for all dancers or all those who wish to experience and practice life as a dance.

BONE MARROW NEI KUNG

In many indigenous cultures, bones are considered especially sacred and are, even long after a person has died, preserved with great care, as they are believed to contain the spirit of the person as well as the spirits of his or her ancestors. It would seem as if people intuitively knew that the bones are the generators of the substance of life and need therefore a special attitude of reverence.

Bone Marrow Nei Kung ("Nei Kung" means awareness or meditative practice), until quite recently a highly guarded secret practice, has always been seen as a vital key to grounding and embodying the life of the spirit in the body. Bone Marrow Nei Kung, by gentle Chi pressure and infusing the bones with Chi, serves to regenerate them by renewing the blood. It requires a form of deep sensing meditation that can only be realized in a state of deep relaxation. Through this practice, even the hardest elements in our body yield to the force of the gentle, as stone yields to water. To enhance the body's receptivity to the electromagnetic forces of the sun, moon, planets, stars, and earth, the bones are first "washed" through special Chi circulation exercises. Through Bone Marrow Nei Kung, Chi in and around the bones can be significantly increased or even doubled. (A thorough discussion of these practices is presented in *Bone Marrow Nei Kung* by Mantak Chia.)

It has been discovered that the bones in the body that form its central axis have a crystal structure that facilitates the body's receptivity to the electromagnetic power entering from the electromagnetic fields of the universe. The body generates and enhances itself as an electromagnetic field.

The more our bones and joints are alive and filled with the bio-electromagnetic Chi, and the more its vibrations increase, the more we feel alive and naturally bounce between heaven and earth. Like our organs and glands, our bones are centers of consciousness, connecting us with earth and heaven.

To move the bones from within and from without is very good. Taoist meditation always seeks a balance between stillness and motion, with awareness, because they are a unity of opposites. Yang can only come about because of yin, and yin can only arise thanks to yang. Actually yin is contained in yang and yang in yin.

Chi acts as a softening cushion between the bones so that they can smoothly turn and do not grind against each other, as happens when they have dried out and lost their softness. As the bones and joints regenerate through various forms of Chi Kung practice, Chi fluids are brought into them and between them. Chi may be viewed as oil which greases a lock or a motor to make it work smoothly again.

It should be remembered that the sockets of the hipbones carry the whole body and its weight and that it is often due to overweight that problems start. Another cause of the absence of Chi fluids between the bones is emotional imbalance and the predominance of negative emotions like depression and anger. These play a critical role. The smooth rotation of the hips over time is directly connected to our emotional state, especially as we grow older.

The smooth functioning of the hip joints is crucial in the whole Chi transmission process. The Chi that comes from below has to travel upward. Breathing into the hip joints and sockets, sending love into the bones, and bringing the inward smile into them helps this process. The hip joints play a critical role as conveyors of the upward Chi flow from the earth, and if our body is well aligned, it can then further travel upward.

The joints can produce abundant "saliva," the elixir of life, which is replete with hormones and contains a variety of precious substances essential for our vitality. Afflictions like arthritis and rheumatism may be overcome by the loving use of consciousness and Chi breathing instead of by conventional medical treatment.

Closing the Three Gates

In order to create and maintain the correct pressure in the lower Tan Tien, we must be able to tighten and seal the sexual organ, the perineum, and the anus. In order to do this, we must be able to contract the pelvic floor and be able to tighten the sexual organ, perineum, and anus in a controlled and coordinated manner. This ability prevents leakage of sexual essence/generative energy (Jing) and preserves it so that it may be transformed into vital life force energy and spirit energy. Tightening and sealing the sexual organ, the perineum, and the anus is called "the closing of the three gates."

The perineum is known as the "gate of life and death" as it plays such a crucial role both in preventing degeneration and in activating all the organs, glands, and other body functions. The perineum—called the Hui Yin—is located between the genitals and the anus. It constitutes the lowest point of the yin or descending energy channels, and is the lower meeting point of the Governor (ascending) Channel and the Functional (descending) Channel. Through the legs and feet, it is the main link with the earth Chi. When the perineum is strong, the organs remain firm and healthy; when it is weak the organs lose cohesiveness and Chi energy drains away.

The ability to achieve control over the three gates and to lead the energy up and inward rather than allowing it to flow down and outward is very important in Tan Tien Chi Kung, as well as the Microcosmic Orbit and Healing Love practices. The dense form of Chi (Jing) produced in the sexual organ is brought into the loop of the Governor and the Functional Channels and thence upward into the brain. On its upward journey, the Chi undergoes several transformations and nourishes and activates all the organs before it finally brings fresh energy and hormones to the brain.

A good beginning practice as we learn to control the three gates is massaging the perineum. Massaging the perineum vitalizes the sexual organs and strengthens the pelvic floor. It also contributes to activating the pineal gland, to which it has a direct connection through the Thrusting Channel, the energy channel that is located in the center of the body between the perineum and the crown. Perineum massage also helps one to become aware of the unity of high and low in one's body. It acknowledges the most honorable function of what are often called "the lower organs."

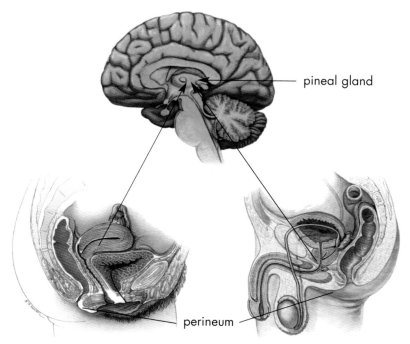

THE PERINEUM AND PINEAL GLAND ARE CONNECTED
THROUGH THE THRUSTING CHANNEL

Contracting the muscles of the perineum, sexual organs, and anus activates our connection with the earth energy. By pulling up these areas and drawing in energy through the soles of the feet, we immediately become grounded and energized. Holding a very gentle contraction in the muscles of the perineum, sexual organs, and anus will keep you grounded during Chi Kung practice.

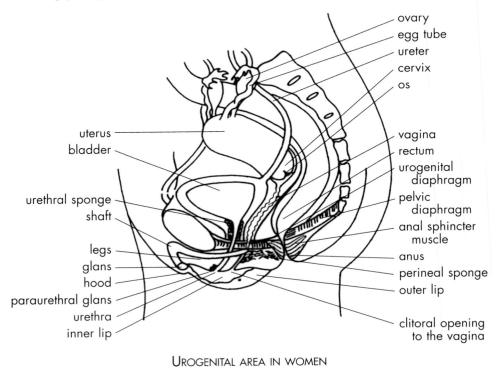

UROGENITAL AREA IN WOMEN

Tightening the perineum and anus strengthens the pelvic and urogenital diaphragm, and holds up and reactivates the organs in the lower Tan Tien, thereby revitalizing them. If coordinated with the downward pressure of the chest diaphragm, it helps to provide the space in which the process of Chi compression can be realized.

As we practice contracting the perineum, sexual organs, and anus, Chi is pressed inward from all sides, and Chi pressure in the lower Tan Tien rises. The more the Chi is concentrated, the higher its

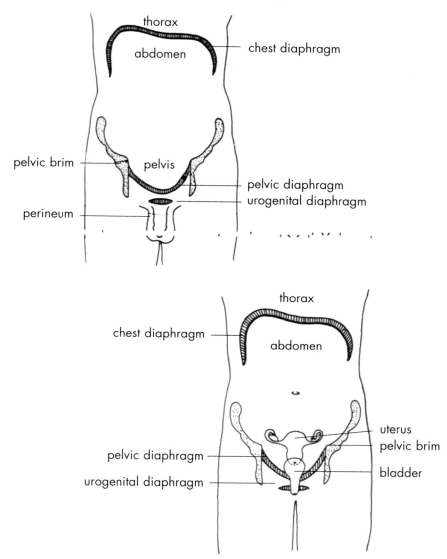

PELVIC AND UROGENITAL DIAPHRAGMS IN MEN AND WOMEN

expansive potential becomes. This practice has been called the creation of a "Chi ball." Scattered Chi is concentrated and compressed in the lower Tan Tien, which raises the inner power needed to activate the whole body and all its flows and networks.

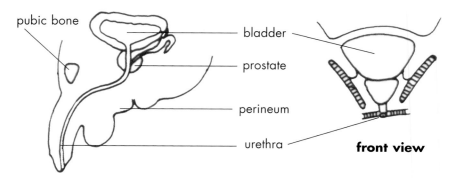

side cross-section

front view

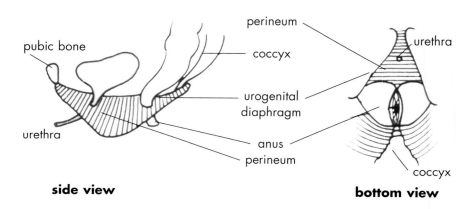

side view

bottom view

THE UROGENITAL AREA IN MEN

ANUS-BODY CONNECTIONS

The anus exercises are important keys of Tan Tien Chi Kung. These exercises strengthen, tighten, and seal the abdomen to prevent leakage of energy. Smiling into the anus is a very im portant practice, as is contraction of the anus: both facilitate energizing all organs in the body. The spiritual energy hidden in the smile helps to raise the quality of the energy and consciousness condensed in the organs and glands.

The Taoists divide the anus into five parts: middle, front, back, left, and right. Each part of the anus has an important energy connection with different parts of the body. The following diagrams illustrate the various anus-body connections.

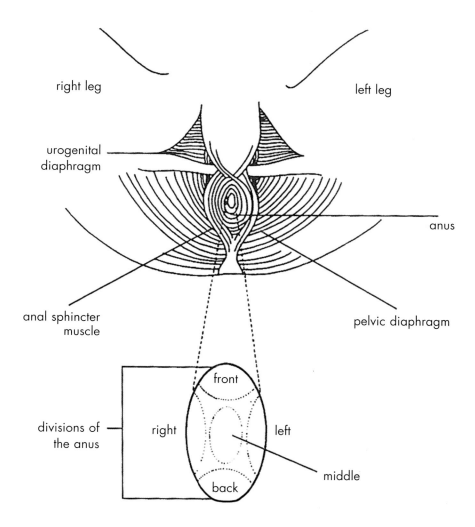

right leg

left leg

urogenital diaphragm

anus

anal sphincter muscle

pelvic diaphragm

divisions of the anus

front

right

left

middle

back

FIVE REGIONS OF THE ANUS

anus and front side of abdominal

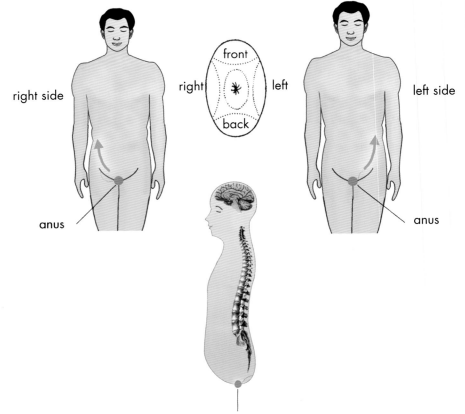

right side

right | left

left side

anus

anus

anus and backside

ANUS AND PERINEUM

The middle part of the anus connects to the organs in the front part of the abdominal area. For women, this connects to the vagina-uterus, for men the prostate gland. It also connects to the aorta and vena cava, stomach, heart, thyroid and parathyroid, pituitary gland, pineal gland, and the top of the head—through the center channel.

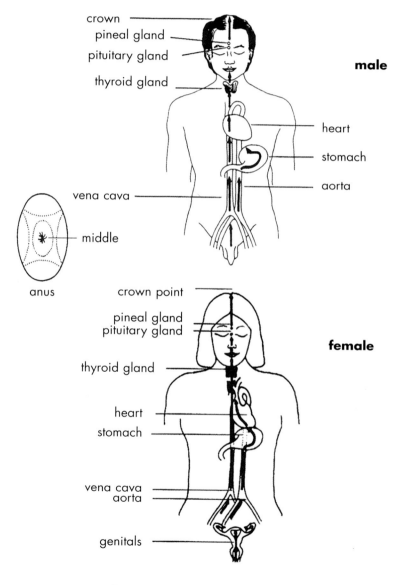

CONNECTIONS OF THE MIDDLE ANUS

The front of the anus connects to the prostate, bladder, small intestine, thymus, thyroid, and brain. As you contract the anus, pull the middle part of the anus up toward the front.

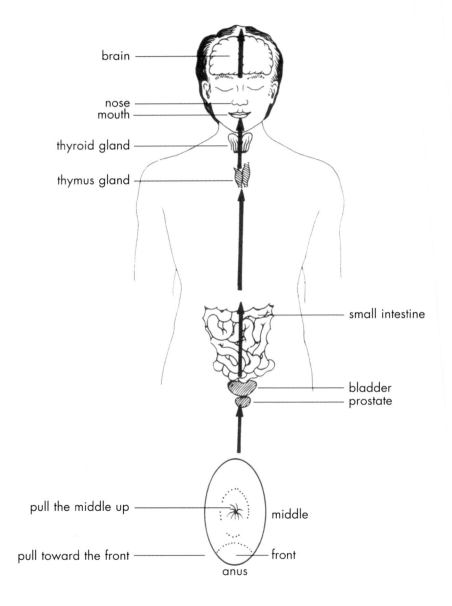

CONNECTIONS OF THE FRONT ANUS

The back of the anus is connected to the coccyx, the sacrum, the back of the spine, and the cerebellum at the base of the skull, also known as the "jade pillow." As you contract the anus, next pull the middle part of the anus up toward the back, toward the sacrum.

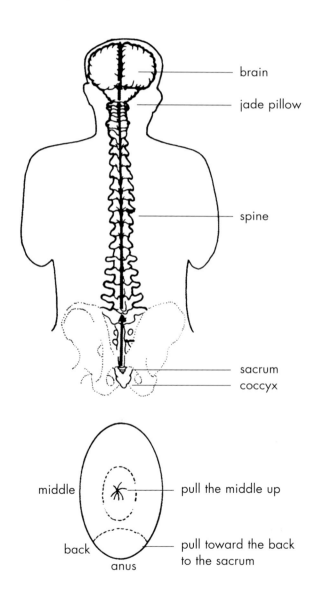

CONNECTIONS OF THE BACK ANUS

The right side of the anus is connected with the right side of the abdomen, the right ovary or right testicle, ascending colon, right kidney, adrenal gland, liver, gall bladder, right lung, and right hemisphere of the brain. As you contract the anus, next pull up the middle and then toward the right side.

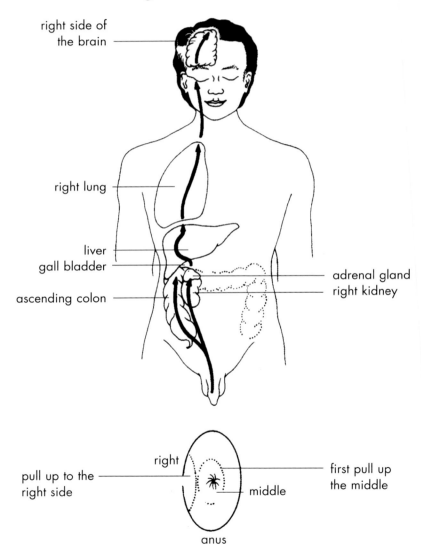

right side of the brain

right lung

liver
gall bladder

ascending colon

adrenal gland
right kidney

right

pull up to the right side

first pull up the middle

middle

anus

CONNECTIONS OF THE RIGHT ANUS (MALE)

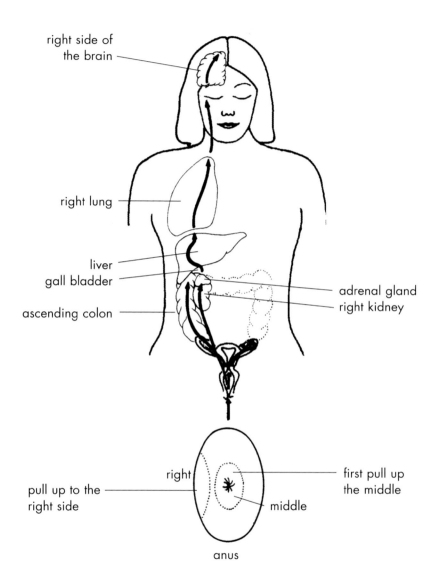

right side of
the brain

right lung

liver
gall bladder

ascending colon

adrenal gland
right kidney

right

pull up to the
right side

first pull up
the middle

middle

anus

Connections of the Right Anus (Female)

The left side of the anus is connected with the left side of the abdomen, the left ovary or left testicle, descending colon, left kidney, adrenal gland, spleen, stomach, left lung, and left hemisphere of the brain. As you contract the anus, next pull up the middle and then toward the left side.

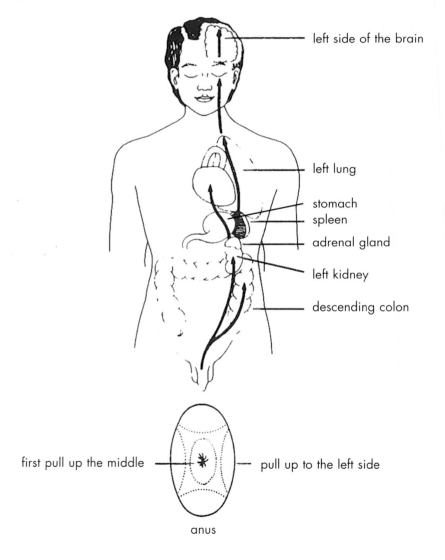

CONNECTIONS OF THE LEFT ANUS (MALE)

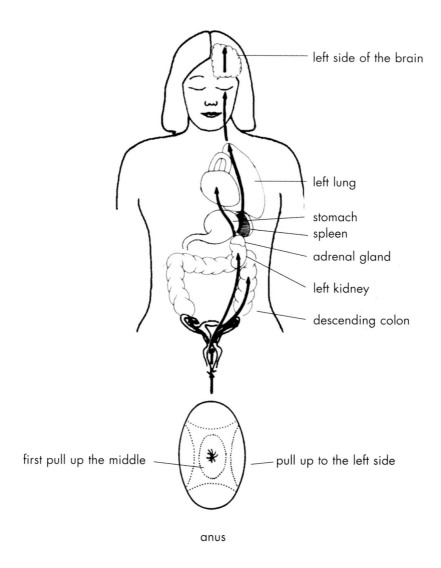

left side of the brain

left lung

stomach

spleen

adrenal gland

left kidney

descending colon

first pull up the middle

pull up to the left side

anus

CONNECTIONS OF THE LEFT ANUS (FEMALE)

In Tan Tien Chi Kung we strengthen all these parts of the anus and develop "perineum power" by contracting and pulling up these areas. When your pelvic area is strong, no energy will leak out of the "three gates," and you can enhance the Chi pressure in your Tan Tien. With a weak perineum and anus, this is not possible.

There are good Taoist exercises to strengthen the different parts of the anus (perineum/pelvic floor) and to learn to contract them without tightening the muscles too much. To make them very strong, which means giving the muscles a strong tonicity, you must do these exercises many times a day. The pleasant thing about them is that you can do these exercises everywhere; good times and places to practice are while waiting at the post office, the bus station, the shop, when you watch a movie or TV, or work on the computer. When you are creative, you will find many occasions during the day to practice these exercises.

The best way to do these exercises is in the standing position. However, you also can practice them sitting or laying on the ground, in bed, or even in the bathtub. We will further discuss exercises to build perineum power in the next chapter.

Empty Force and Perineum Power

BUILDING PRESSURE IN THE LOWER TAN TIEN

In this chapter we will discuss a number of exercises for building Chi pressure in the lower Tan Tien through contraction of the anus and perineum and working with the breath and chest diaphragm.

There are seven important areas in the lower Tan Tien where we would like to develop Chi pressure:

- below the navel (also known as the Chi Hai or "ocean of Chi")
- lowest part of the abdomen (bladder area)
- above the navel (solar plexus area)
- both left and right sides of the lower Tan Tien
- both left and right sides of the body
- both kidneys
- the Ming Men point (also known as the "door of life," located between the third and forth lumbar vertebrae, just beneath the two kidneys, and opposite the navel).

Just as with a balloon you can press on one side of the balloon to increase the pressure on the other side, in a similar way, you can press or contract one area of the abdominal/lower Tan Tien region to increase pressure in other parts.

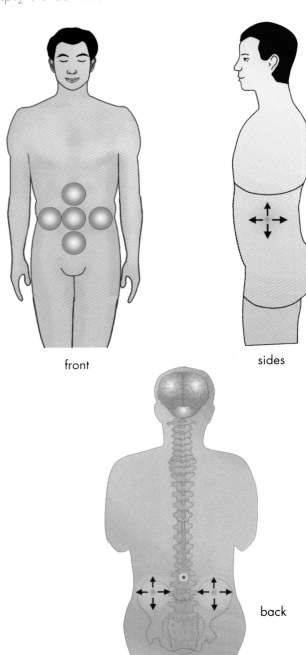

front

sides

back

AREAS TO DEVELOP CHI PRESSURE

There are two main contracting actions in which to do this: pulling up the perineum and anus (discussed in the previous chapter), and pressing down the chest diaphragm. When you press down the chest diaphragm, press in and down all along the edge of the rib cage. Through these contracting actions, the chest diaphragm, abdominal wall, and perineum press into the abdominal cavity. This will reduce the space in the lower Tan Tien region and condense the Chi in this area, creating a "Chi ball."

While you pull up on the perineum and anus and press down on the chest diaphragm, there are two corresponding breathing actions. First, take one quick, deep breath to expand the abdomen. Then exhale, expelling the breath. Without inhaling, further contract the abdomen, squeezing up and in. In this way, you are "inhaling without inhaling" and drawing Chi into the abdomen (see figure on page 72). The principle involved in this special breathing practice is called "Empty Force," and is central to all the Tan Tien Chi Kung practices that induce Chi compression in the lower Tan Tien. A variation of this practice is presented in detail in the upcoming discussion of the Dragon and Tiger Breath practice.

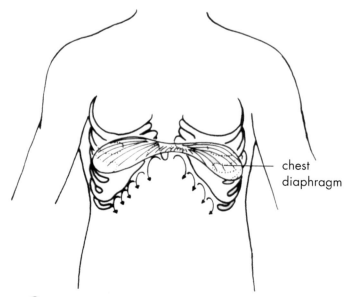

chest diaphragm

CONTRACTING AND RELAXING THE CHEST DIAPHRAGM

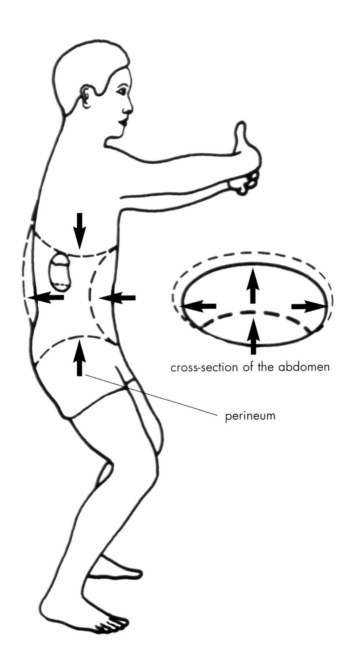

cross-section of the abdomen

perineum

CONTRACTING THE LOWER TAN TIEN REGION

PERINEUM POWER EXERCISES

Dragon and Tiger Breath

In the following exercise, we build Chi in the Chi Hai (the area below the navel) through contracting the anus and perineum and practicing several special forms of breathing. The dragon and tiger breaths are used in many of the perineum power exercises.

1. First, stand with the feet parallel and shoulder width apart. All the nine points of the feet (see below) should be firmly rooted in the earth.

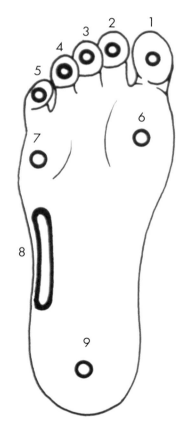

ROOT THE NINE POINTS OF THE FOOT IN THE EARTH

2. Keep part of the awareness on the anus, perineum, and sexual organs.

3. Put your hands on the Chi Hai, below the navel on the lower abdomen, very gently and softly (see figure below). Smile and do a few deep, abdominal breaths.

navel

PLACE HANDS ON THE CHI HAI, BELOW THE NAVEL ON THE LOWER ABDOMEN

4. Exhale and flatten and contract the abdominal area. Follow this action with the fingers of both hands.

5. Next, inhale with a half breath, using the dragon sound. The dragon sound is a high-pitched *Hummmmmm*. Feel a pressure, like that of a vacuum cleaner, in the abdominal area and the throat. This vacuum/sucking sensation is a sucking in of Chi pressure.

6. Lightly pull up the anus, perineum, and sexual organs. At the same time, expand the abdomen, while holding the breath and Chi pressure in the Chi Hai. Always keep the chest diaphragm down and the chest relaxed.

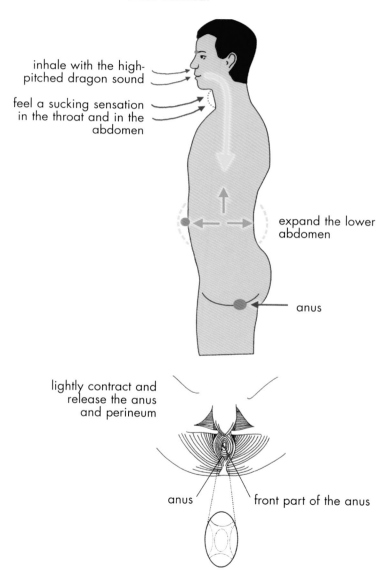

inhale with the high-pitched dragon sound

feel a sucking sensation in the throat and in the abdomen

expand the lower abdomen

anus

lightly contract and release the anus and perineum

anus

front part of the anus

DRAGON BREATH

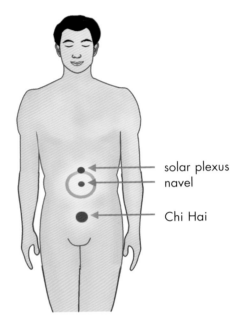

solar plexus
navel

Chi Hai

SOLAR PLEXUS, NAVEL, AND CHI HAI AREAS

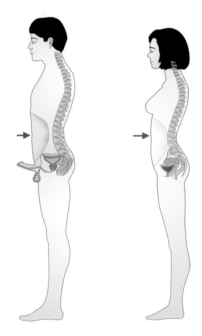

POSITION OF THE CHI HAI IN MEN AND WOMEN

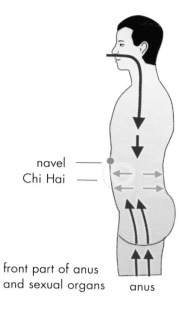

navel ——

Chi Hai ——

front part of anus
and sexual organs   anus

BUILD AND HOLD THE PRESSURE IN THE CHI HAI

7. Now, exhale with the tiger sound. The tiger sound, *Hummmmmm*, is a low-pitched, growling sound. Push the energy pressure down to the lower abdominal area.

EXHALE WITH THE TIGER SOUND AND PUSH THE CHI PRESSURE
DOWN INTO THE LOWER ABDOMEN

8. Next, hold the breath out and laugh softly inside. Feel the vibration in the Chi Hai. Hold the breath out as long as is comfortable, then inhale and slowly regulate the breath.

FEEL THE VIBRATION IN THE CHI HAI

9. Repeat the whole process of the dragon and tiger breath three to six times. Feel the pressure becoming stronger with every breath. When you inhale and exhale consciously, you draw in and hold Chi. When you inhale and exhale unconsciously, you lose Chi.

Bladder Area Exercise

In this exercise, we focus on the lowest region of the abdomen, including the bladder and, for women, the uterus.

1. First, stand with the feet parallel and shoulder width apart. All the nine points of the feet should be firmly rooted in the earth.
2. Keep part of the awareness on the middle part, the front part, and the back part of the anus as well as the perineum. For women, keep part of the awareness in the uterus; for men, the prostate gland.
3. Place your hands on the Chi Hai, below the navel on the lower abdomen. Smile and do a few deep, abdominal breaths.

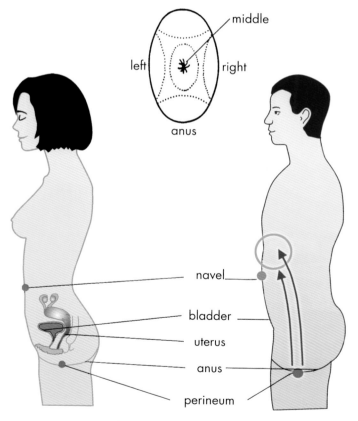

ANUS, BLADDER, UTERUS

4. Exhale and flatten and contract the abdominal area. Follow this action with the fingers of both hands.

5. Hold the breath out for a short while. Lightly suck and contract the abdomen up and in. Feel the suction inside.

6. Inhale one third of the breath with the high-pitched, dragon sound. Feel the vacuum pressure in the abdomen and throat, sucking in Chi pressure. At the same time, contract and pull up the anus.

7. Inhale the second third of the breath. Contract, pulling up the front part of the anus and the sexual organs toward the bladder/ uterus and lowest part of the abdomen. Expand the abdomen.

CONTRACT THE ABDOMEN

FEEL THE VACUUM PRESSURE

8. Inhale the last third of the breath and contract and pull up more of the front part of the anus toward the bladder and uterus. At the same time, push the lower abdominal area out against the fingers.

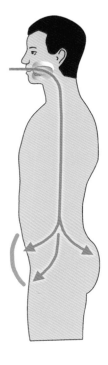

TONGUE AGAINST THE PALATE,
PRESS THE LOWER ABDOMEN
OUT AS YOU INHALE

EXHALE WITH THE
KIDNEY SOUND

9. Keep your tongue against the palate. Hold the breath in as long as you feel comfortable.

10. Now, exhale with the kidney sound *Choooooo*. When you do this well, the coccyx will lightly turn in and the sacrum will push out, rounding the lower back, because the sacrum and the sexual organs are connected. Repeat this entire practice three to six times, Feel the pressure becoming stronger with every breath. Then relax and let go, smiling into the entire lower abdomen. Feel Chi and blood flow into the area.

Solar Plexus Area Exercise

In this exercise, we focus on the solar plexus region.

1. First, stand with the feet parallel and shoulder width apart. All the nine points of the feet should be firmly rooted in the earth.
2. Keep part of the awareness on the middle and front part of the anus as well as the perineum. For women, keep part of the awareness in the uterus; for men, the prostate gland.
3. Place your hands on the solar plexus, above the below the navel. Smile and do a few deep, abdominal breaths.
4. Exhale and flatten and contract the abdominal area. Follow this action with the fingers of both hands.

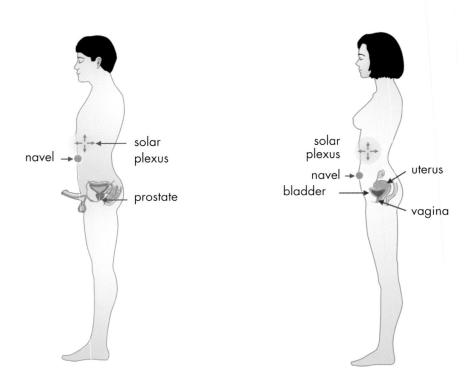

SOLAR PLEXUS IN MEN AND WOMEN

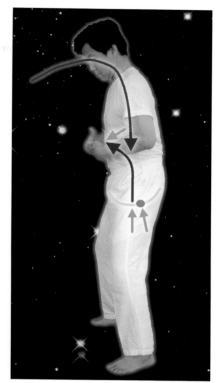

CONTRACT THE ABDOMEN AND PULL UP THE ANUS

5. Hold the breath out for a short while. Lightly suck and contract the abdomen up and in. Feel the suction inside.

6. Inhale one third of the breath with the high-pitched, dragon sound. Feel the vacuum pressure in the abdomen and throat, sucking in Chi pressure.

7. Inhale the second third of the breath. At the same time, contract and pull up the anus. Pull up the front part of the anus and the sexual organs toward the solar plexus. While you are doing this, expand and push the navel area out.

8. Inhale the last third of the breath and contract and pull up more of the front part of the anus toward the solar plexus. At the same time, push the solar plexus area out against the fingers.

9. Keep your tongue against the palate. Hold the breath in as long as you feel comfortable.

10. Now, exhale with the kidney sound *Choooooo*. When you do this well, the coccyx will lightly turn in and the sacrum will push out, rounding the lower back, because the sacrum and the sexual organs are connected. Repeat this entire practice three to six times. Feel the pressure becoming stronger with every breath. Then relax and let go, smiling into the entire abdomen region, particularly the solar plexus. Feel Chi and blood flow into the area.

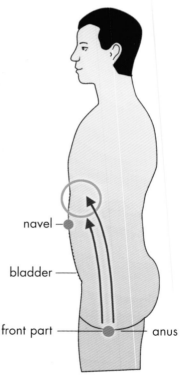

navel
bladder
front part — anus

EXHALE WITH ANUS AND PERINEUM POWER

ANUS AND SOLAR PLEXUS
CONNECTIONS

Bladder Area Exercise #2

In this exercise, we modify the preceding bladder area exercise, inhaling with one slow breath rather than three short breaths.

1. First, stand with the feet parallel and shoulder width apart. All the nine points of the feet should be firmly rooted in the earth.
2. Keep part of the awareness on the middle part, the front part, and the back part of the anus as well as the perineum. For women, keep part of the awareness in the uterus; for men, the prostate gland.
3. Place your hands on the Chi Hai, below the navel on the lower abdomen. Exhale and flatten and contract the abdominal area. Use the fingers to press into the Chi Hai.

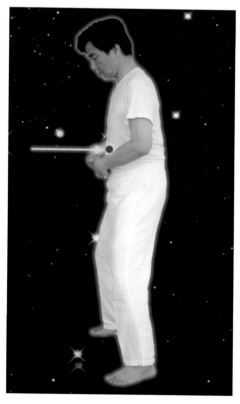

PLACE THE HANDS ON THE CHI HAI

4. Hold the breath out for a short while. Lightly suck and contract the abdomen up and in. Feel the suction inside.

5. Inhale with one long, slow breath. At the same time, contract and pull up the front part of the anus and the sexual organs toward the bladder/uterus and lowest part of the abdomen. At the same time, expand the abdomen, pushing the lower abdominal area out against the fingers.

6. Hold the breath in as long as you feel comfortable, then exhale and rest. Repeat this process three to six times.

Exercise for the Sides of the Lower Tan Tien

In this exercise, we focus on the right and left sides of the lower Tan Tien.

1. Begin standing with the feet parallel and shoulder width apart. All the nine points of the feet should be firmly rooted in the earth.

2. Keep part of the awareness on the middle part and the left and right sides of the anus as well as the perineum. For women, keep part of the awareness in the uterus; for men, the prostate gland.

3. Place your fingers on both left and right sides of the front part of the lower Tan Tien. Smile and do a few deep, abdominal breaths.

4. Hold the breath out for a short while. Lightly suck and contract the abdomen up and in. Feel the suction inside.

6. Now inhale half the breath with the high-pitched dragon sound. Feel the vacuum pressure in the abdomen and throat, sucking Chi pressure in.

7. At the same time, contract and pull up on the left and right sides of the anus.

8. Inhale the other half of the breath with the high-pitched dragon sound. Contract and pull more of the left and right sides of the anus up toward the left and right sides of the lower Tan Tien. At the same time, push the left and right sides of the lower Tan Tien out against your fingers.

EXHALE AND PRESS IN WITH THE FINGERS ON
THE SIDES OF THE LOWER TAN TIEN

9. Hold the breath in as long as is comfortable, maintaining the
   Chi pressure. Always keep the chest diaphragm down and the
   chest relaxed.
10. Exhale with the low-pitched, growling tiger sound. Push the
    energy pressure out to both sides. Laugh softly inside and feel a
    vibration in the Chi Hai and in both sides of the lower Tan Tien.
    Hold the breath out as long as is comfortable.

11. Then inhale slowly and relax, smiling into the entire abdominal region, particularly the two sides of the lower Tan Tien. Repeat this practice three to six times, feeling the energy pressure becoming stronger with every breath. Feel Chi and blood flow into the area.

LAUGH SOFTLY INSIDE AND FEEL A VIBRATION
IN BOTH SIDES OF THE LOWER TAN TIEN

Exercise for the Sides of the Body

In this exercise, we focus on the right and left sides of body.

1. Begin standing with the feet parallel and shoulder width apart. All the nine points of the feet should be firmly rooted in the earth.

2. Keep part of the awareness on the middle part and the left and right sides of the anus as well as the perineum. For women, keep part of the awareness in the uterus; for men, the prostate gland.

3. Place your hands gently on the left and right sides of your body.

PLACE THE HANDS ON THE LEFT AND RIGHT SIDES OF THE BODY

4. Exhale and flatten and contract the abdominal area. Use the fingers to press into the sides.

5. Hold the breath out for a short while. Lightly suck and contract the abdomen up and in. Feel the suction inside.

6. Now inhale half the breath with the high-pitched dragon sound. Feel the vacuum pressure in the abdomen and throat, sucking Chi pressure in.

MAKE THE DRAGON SOUND AS YOU INHALE HALF THE BREATH

7. At the same time, contract and pull up on the left and right sides of the anus.

8. Inhale the other half of the breath with the high-pitched dragon sound. Contract and pull up more of the left and right sides of the anus toward the left and right sides of the body. At the same time, push the left and right sides of the body out against your fingers. Feel both sides expanding.

9. Hold the breath in as long as is comfortable, maintaining the Chi pressure. Always keep the chest diaphragm down and the chest relaxed.

10. Now, exhale with the low-pitched, growling tiger sound. Slowly and consciously, push the Chi pressure out to both sides. Maintain equal force on both sides.

COMPLETE THE DRAGON IN-BREATH
AND PUSH OUT ON THE LEFT AND
RIGHT SIDES OF THE BODY

EXHALE WITH THE TIGER SOUND,
CONTINUING TO EXPAND TO THE
LEFT AND RIGHT

11. Laugh softly inside and feel a vibration throughout the lower Tan Tien. Hold the breath out as long as is comfortable.

12. Then inhale slowly and relax, smiling into the entire abdominal region, particularly the two sides of the body. Repeat this practice three to six times, feeling the energy pressure becoming stronger with every breath. Feel Chi and blood flow into the area.

Kidneys Exercise

In this exercise, we focus on the right and left sides of kidneys.

1. Begin standing with the feet parallel and shoulder width apart. All the nine points of the feet should be firmly rooted in the earth.
2. Keep part of the awareness on the middle part and the left and right sides of the anus as well as the perineum. For women, keep part of the awareness in the uterus; for men, the prostate gland.
3. Place your hands gently on your left and right kidneys. Your spine should slightly arch.
4. Exhale and flatten and contract the abdominal area.

PLACE THE HANDS ON THE LEFT AND RIGHT KIDNEYS

5. Hold the breath out for a short while. Lightly suck and contract the abdomen up and in. Feel the suction inside. Smile to the kidneys.

6. Now inhale half the breath with the high-pitched dragon sound. Feel the vacuum pressure in the abdomen and throat, sucking Chi pressure in.

7. At the same time, contract and pull up on the left and right sides of the anus.

8. Inhale the other half of the breath with the high-pitched dragon sound. Contract and pull up more of the left and right sides of the anus toward the left and right kidneys. At the same time, lightly round the back and press out against your hands.

9. Feel the kidneys expanding, and the whole lumbar area opening.

COMPLETE THE DRAGON IN-BREATH AND FEEL THE KIDNEY AREA EXPANDING AND THE WHOLE LUMBAR AREA OPENING

10. Hold the breath in as long as is comfortable, maintaining the Chi pressure. Always keep the chest diaphragm down and the chest relaxed.

11. Now, exhale with the low-pitched, growling tiger sound. Slowly and consciously, push the Chi pressure out to both kidneys and the lower abdomen as you exhale. Maintain equal force on both sides.

12. Laugh softly inside and feel a vibration throughout the lower Tan Tien. Hold the breath out as long as is comfortable.

13. Then inhale slowly and relax, smiling into the entire abdominal region, particularly the kidneys. Repeat this practice three to six times, feeling the energy pressure becoming stronger with every breath. Feel a strong Chi "belt" around your waist. This exercise will strengthen the kidneys and increase your original force.

EXHALE WITH THE TIGER SOUND, CONTINUING TO
PUSH THE CHI PRESSURE OUT TO BOTH KIDNEYS

Door of Life Exercise

In this exercise, we focus on the door of life, also known as the Ming Men. The door of life is located between the third and forth lumbar vertebrae, just beneath the two kidneys, and opposite the navel.

1. Begin standing with the feet parallel and shoulder width apart. All the nine points of the feet should be firmly rooted in the earth.
2. Keep part of the awareness on the middle part and the left and right sides of the anus as well as the perineum. For women, keep part of the awareness in the uterus; for men, the prostate gland.
3. Place your hands gently over the door of life area, with the palms covering the kidneys. Your spine should arch slightly forward.

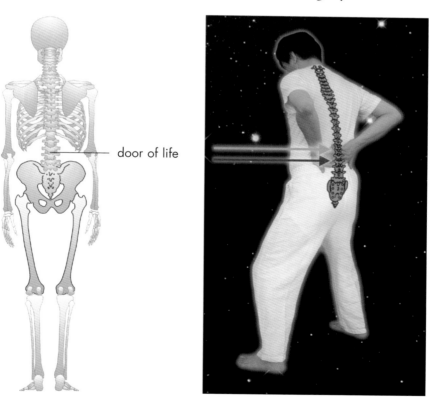

door of life

PLACE THE HANDS ON THE DOOR OF LIFE

4. Exhale and flatten and contract the abdominal area.

5. Hold the breath out for a short while. Lightly suck and contract the abdomen up and in. Feel the suction inside. Smile to the door of life.

6. Now inhale half the breath with the high-pitched dragon sound. Feel the vacuum pressure in the abdomen and throat, sucking Chi pressure in.

7. At the same time, contract and pull up on the anus, particularly the center and back side of the anus. Be aware of the soles of your feet, the coccyx, and the sacrum. As you pull up the back part of the anus, feel the pulsation in the door of life sucking up the energy of the earth and moving it upward through the spine to the brain.

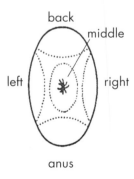

back

middle

left

right

anus

COMPLETE THE DRAGON IN-BREATH AND FEEL THE DOOR OF LIFE
AREA EXPANDING AND THE WHOLE LUMBAR AREA OPENING

8. Inhale the other half of the breath with the high-pitched dragon sound. Contract and pull up more anus. At the same time, lightly round the back and press the energy out against your hands.

9. Feel the door of life expanding, and the whole lumbar area opening.

10. Hold the breath in as long as is comfortable, maintaining the Chi pressure. Always keep the chest diaphragm down and the chest relaxed.

11. Now, exhale with the low-pitched, growling tiger sound. Slowly and consciously, push the Chi pressure out the door of life as you exhale. Maintain steady force.

EXHALE WITH THE TIGER SOUND, PUSHING THE CHI
PRESSURE OUT TO THE DOOR OF LIFE AREA

12. Laugh softly inside and feel a vibration throughout the lower Tan Tien. Hold the breath out as long as is comfortable.
13. Then inhale slowly and relax, smiling into the entire abdominal region, particularly the door of life.
14. Now, exhale again, putting both feet together. Place the palms over the navel while focusing on the door of life.
15. Repeat the whole sequence three to six times, feeling the energy pressure becoming stronger with every breath, the door of life open and breathing, and the entire abdomen full of Chi and pulsating.

Chest Exercise

In this exercise, we focus on the chest region.

1. Begin standing with the feet parallel and shoulder width apart. All the nine points of the feet should be firmly rooted in the earth.
2. Keep part of the awareness on the middle, front, left, and right parts of the anus as well as the perineum. For women, keep part of the awareness in the uterus; for men, the prostate gland.
3. Place your hands gently on both sides of the chest, with thumbs under the armpits.
4. Exhale and flatten the chest.
5. Hold the breath out for a short while. Lightly suck and contract the abdomen up and in. Feel the suction inside. Smile to the entire chest area.
6. Now inhale half the breath with the high-pitched dragon sound. Feel the vacuum pressure in the abdomen and throat, sucking Chi pressure in.
7. At the same time, contract and pull up the front part of the anus and expand the whole front part of the lower Tan Tien.
8. Inhale the other half of the breath with the high-pitched dragon sound. Contract and pull the left and right sides of the anus up

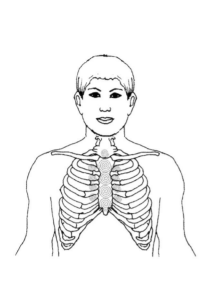

PLACE THE HANDS ON THE CHEST

toward the left and right rib cage. Let the Chi expand and round the upper back.

9. Hold the breath in as long as is comfortable, maintaining the Chi pressure. Always keep the chest diaphragm down and the chest relaxed.

10. Now, exhale with the low-pitched, growling tiger sound. Slowly and consciously, push the Chi pressure down to the lower abdomen and then let the pressure from the lower abdomen expand up to the upper chest. Feel the whole chest and lower Tan Tien area expanding.

11. Laugh softly inside and feel a vibration throughout the lower Tan Tien. Hold the breath out as long as is comfortable.

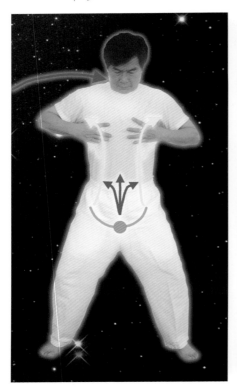

COMPLETE THE DRAGON IN-BREATH AND
FEEL THE CHEST EXPANDING AND UPPER
BACK OPENING

EXHALE WITH THE TIGER SOUND,
PUSHING THE CHI PRESSURE DOWN
TO THE LOWER ABDOMEN

12. Then inhale slowly and relax, smiling into the entire chest
    region, particularly the door of life.
13. Repeat the whole sequence three to six times, feeling the energy
    pressure becoming stronger with every breath.

Total Tan Tien Breathing

This exercise combines all of the preceding exercise into one.

1. Begin standing with the feet parallel and shoulder width apart. All
   the nine points of the feet should be firmly rooted in the earth.

2. Keep part of the awareness on the anus and perineum. For women, keep part of the awareness in the uterus; for men, the prostate gland.

3. Breathe slowly and deeply until you feel nice and calm.

4. Smile and gently place both hands on the lower Tan Tien.

5. Exhale and flatten and contract the abdominal area.

6. Hold the breath out for a short while. Lightly suck and contract the abdomen up and in. Feel the suction inside. Smile to the entire lower Tan Tien area.

7. Now inhale half the breath with the high-pitched dragon sound. Feel the vacuum pressure in the abdomen and throat, sucking Chi pressure in.

8. At the same time, contract and pull up on the anus. Pull the front, left, and right sides of the anus up toward the front, left, and right sides of the abdomen.

COMPLETE THE DRAGON IN-BREATH AND FEEL THE ENTIRE ABDOMEN AND LOWER TAN TIEN AREA EXPANDING

9. Expand and push out the lower part of the navel and the upper, left, and right sides of the abdomen. You can move your fingers along each part that you expand.

10. Inhale the other half of the breath with the high-pitched dragon sound. Contract and pull the left, right, and back sides of the anus up toward the left and right sides of the kidneys and the door of life.

11. Feel the entire lower Tan Tien area expanding.

12. Hold the breath in as long as is comfortable, maintaining the Chi pressure. Always keep the chest diaphragm down and the chest relaxed.

13. Now, exhale with the low-pitched, growling tiger sound. Slowly and consciously, push the Chi pressure outward into the entire abdomen. Maintain steady force.

14. Laugh softly inside and feel a vibration throughout the lower Tan Tien. Hold the breath out as long as is comfortable.

15. Then inhale slowly and relax, smiling into the entire abdominal region.

16. Repeat the whole sequence three to six times, feeling the energy pressure becoming stronger with every breath, and the entire abdomen full of Chi and pulsating.

Exercises to Increase Chi Pressure and Vibration

This exercise follows the steps and principles of the previous perineum power exercises, except that this time, you use your fingers and hands to give counter-pressure against the pressure of the Chi from inside.

1. Begin standing with the feet parallel and shoulder width apart. All the nine points of the feet should be firmly rooted in the earth.

2. Keep part of the awareness on the anus and perineum. For women, keep part of the awareness in the uterus; for men, the prostate gland.

3. Breathe slowly and deeply until you feel nice and calm.

4. Place your fingers, your fists, or the edge of your hands on the Chi Hai in the lower abdomen.

5. Exhale and flatten and contract the abdominal area.

6. Hold the breath out for a short while. Lightly suck and contract the abdomen up and in. Feel the suction inside. Smile to the entire lower Tan Tien area.

7. Now inhale, and while you are inhaling, contract and pull up on the anus. Pull the front, left, right, and back sides of the anus up toward the front, left, right, and back sides of the abdomen.

8. Expand and push the energy out the Chi Hai against the pressure of your hands.

9. Slowly exhale, increasing the pressure of your hands. Push the Chi down in the lower abdomen against the pressure of your hands.

PUSH THE ENERGY OUT FROM INSIDE AGAINST THE PRESSURE OF YOUR HANDS

10. You will notice that with the counteracting force of the hands, the internal Chi pressure becomes stronger. Repeat this several times.

11. The last time, exhale quickly with the deep, growling tiger sound, pushing the energy down and out against your hands. The sound is made through a quick expansion from the lower abdomen. The exhalation, expansion, and sound should be completely synchronized.

12. After the last (tiger) exhalation, hold the breath out and tap both fists on the Chi Hai until you feel a vibration in this area.

13. Repeat these steps for each of the other six areas of the lower Tan Tien, continuing to use the hands as a counter-force. (Tapping on the uterus and bladder is especially good for women). Work with each area until you feel a very deep vibration of the Chi inside the lower Tan Tien.

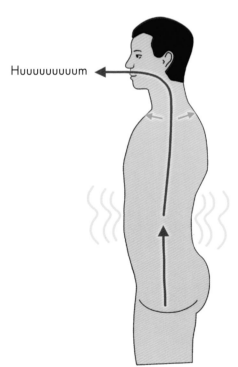

Huuuuuuuuum

EXHALE QUICKLY WITH THE DEEP TIGER SOUND

14. Rest with the palms lightly covering the lower Tan Tien. Feel the Chi in the lower Tan Tien breathing and pulsating.

15. Inhale and pull up the front, back, left, and right parts of the anus together with a light contraction of the eyes and mouth. Feel the suction in the lower Tan Tien, palms, soles of the feet, perineum, sacrum, mid-eyebrow point, and the crown. Exhale and condense the energy in the lower Tan Tien. Repeat this final step several times to safely store the Chi in the lower Tan Tien.

Working with a Partner

You can picture the lower Tan Tien as a balloon that you can fill with air, creating pressure in the balloon. We fill a balloon by blowing air into it little by little. Blow and hold, blow and hold. With the lower Tan Tien it is the same. In this way you can build and maintain the pressure.

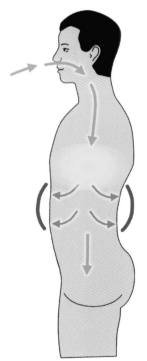

INCREASE CHI PRESSURE WITH EVERY BREATH

Another way to practice building pressure in the lower Tan Tien is to work with the resistance provided by a partner, following the same principles presented in the previous exercise.

1. Stand with your feet shoulder width apart, facing a partner.

USE YOUR PARTNER'S FIST TO BUILD MORE CHI PRESSURE

2. Gently put your fist on your partner's lower Tan Tien.

3. Let your partner inhale into the abdomen and draw Chi into the abdomen. Next, your partner should press Chi out of the Chi Hai area, pushing the abdomen against your fist.

4. Next, your partner should exhale quickly and release the Chi pressure from inside. You will feel that the Chi pressure is gone and that you are pushing into an empty Tan Tien.

5. Have your partner repeat this several times, building pressure by drawing up on the anus and perineum and pushing down on the chest diaphragm with each breath, as explained in the previous exercises. Your partner will build pressure with each breath, just like the balloon. The Chi pressure in the Tan Tan will be more condensed and stronger.

6. As you continue to push into your partner's lower Tan Tien, you will feel that the energy is building in the lower Tan Tien and can be moved around.

7. Let your partner now laugh in the lower Tan Tien while you are still pushing, and you will feel the Chi pressure becoming stronger, moving, and vibrating.

8. Next, change places and let your partner work on you.

RELEASING TENSION IN THE CHEST DIAPHRAGM

Many people have a stiff chest diaphragm that sticks to the rib cage. In order to be able to develop Chi pressure, we should have a chest diaphragm that is loose and that can easily move up and down. To release the tension in the chest diaphragm, you can massage it.

You can massage the chest diaphragm by massaging under and along the rib cage from top to bottom. First, put the middle fingers from the left hand, with the palm facing upward, under the rib cage. Place your right hand on the lower part of the right rib cage and push the rib cage downward with the mouth of your right hand. Repeat for the left side.

This massage will loosen and stretch the chest diaphragm and will facilitate and deepen the breath. It will help you to be able to push the chest diaphragm down on the exhalation, which is necessary in the perineum power exercises for developing Chi pressure in the lower Tan Tien.

MASSAGE CAN RELEASE TENSION IN THE CHEST DIAPHRAGM

The Tan Tien Chi Kung Animal Postures

The practice of Tan Tien Chi Kung typically involves a number of preparatory exercises and the eleven Tan Tien Chi Kung animal postures. In the preceding chapters, we discussed important preparatory practices in which we learn to increase the Chi pressure in the Tan Tien, organs, fascia, lumbar area, and door of life through a combination of breathing, pressing down on the chest diaphragm, and pulling up on the perineum and anus. These introductory exercises also open the sacrum and hip joints, and nourish our original force. In this chapter we will briefly discuss a few warm-up practices, and then proceed with presenting the eleven animal postures.

The animal postures build upon the skills we learn in the preparatory exercises. In fact, they have the same results; however, they are more powerful, and will significantly enhance the Chi pressure in the lower Tan Tien and will strengthen the perineum and rooting power. An open sacrum and a strong anus are necessary conditions for the development of Chi pressure in the lower Tan Tien.

TAN TIEN CHI KUNG WARM-UP

The sacrum, groin area, hip joints, and iliopsoas (hip flexors) all form what is known as the "kua." When the kua is closed, the nerves and the flow of Chi, blood, and lymph fluid up and down the legs is blocked. In order to enable the sacrum to move freely, the sacrum should be able to move separately from the hip bones. When the sacrum and the pelvis are open there is space for the Chi to flow, and we can push the Chi into the lower Tan Tien.

The exercises in the preceding chapter are an excellent way to warm up for the animal postures practice. You can also begin with the following exercise to open the sacrum.

First, stand with the feet shoulder width apart, feet parallel, both big toes slightly turned inward. Place the nine points of the feet firmly on the ground. Gently rub the sacrum area with both hands to stimulate and warm up the sacrum. Then, holding your hands on the sacrum, move the sacrum back and forth.

Now, with your hands at your sides, begin to lightly twist and spiral the ankles and knees in an outward-turning direction. Exhale, pressing the heels firmly into the ground, with the big toes slightly inward. Press the whole legs firmly down into the earth. Continue to

GENTLY RUB THE SACRUM

rotate the leg bones to the outside. This will create a tension in the tendons. It will also make the feet and legs become one piece that attaches to the hip bones. This will help pull open the hips and slightly separate them from the sacrum. When you open the sacrum in this way, it feels like you are pulling the hips to the sides. At the same time, you are also pushing the sacrum to the back, tucking the coccyx in, and opening the pelvis. This will make the whole kua area expand.

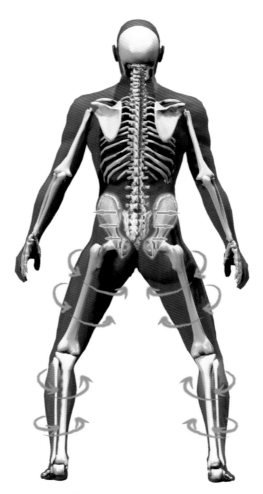

OPENING THE SACRUM

THE ELEVEN ANIMAL POSTURES

For all eleven animal postures, begin standing with the feet parallel and shoulder width apart. Let your arms rest at your sides. All the nine points of the feet should be firmly rooted in the earth. Keep part of your awareness on the anus and perineum, and pull the anus up and in. Keep the chest diaphragm down and the chest relaxed.

Rabbit

The rabbit exercise develops the Chi pressure in the front part of the lower Tan Tien, navel, and pelvic area.

BEGIN ALL ANIMAL POSTURES IN THE BASIC STANDING POSTURE

1. Begin in the basic standing posture.
2. Inhale, pulling up the anus and perineum, simultaneously making the high-pitched dragon sound *hunnnnn*. Feel the vacuum sensation in the lower abdomen and the throat sucking Chi into and expanding the lower abdomen and the throat.
3. At the same time, raise the arms slightly above the head.

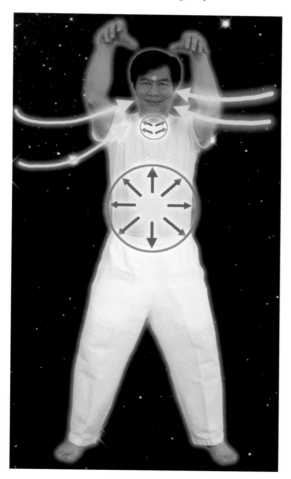

BEGIN RABBIT POSTURE WITH THE DRAGON IN-BREATH

4. Exhale quickly with the low, growling tiger sound *hummmm*.
5. At the same time, pull the front part of the anus up even more and widen your nostrils. Sink down a little in the kua.

6. Press the palms down and out, and push the Chi pressure down into the front part of the lower Tan Tien and the pelvic area with the sound.

7. It is very important that you synchronize these three movements. You will feel the Chi pressure increasing in the lower abdomen, the lower Tan Tien, and the palms of your hands. The kua and

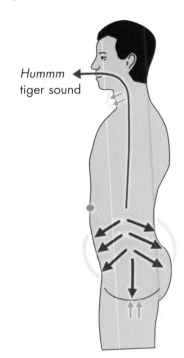

Hummm tiger sound

RABBIT EXHALING WITH TIGER SOUND

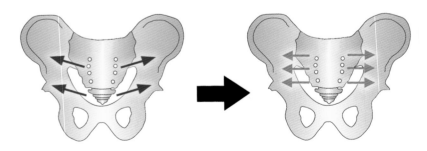

RABBIT POSTURE OPENS THE KUA AND HIP JOINTS

the hip joints will open more due to this Chi pressure.

8. Repeat several times. Complete the exercise with the ending practice discussed at the end of this chapter.

Crane

This exercise develops the Chi pressure in both sides of the lower Tan Tien.

1. Begin in the basic standing posture.
2. Inhale, pulling up the anus and perineum, simultaneously making the high-pitched dragon sound. Feel the vacuum sensation in the lower abdomen and the throat sucking Chi into and expanding the lower abdomen and the throat.
3. At the same time, raise the arms slightly above the head, with the fingers forming a beak.

CRANE RAISES ITS BEAK

4. Exhale quickly with the low, growling tiger sound.

5. At the same time, pull the left and right parts of the anus up even more. Sink down a little in the kua.

6. Press the palms down to hip level and then press the hands out to the sides. Push the Chi pressure down and out into the left and right sides of the lower Tan Tien with the sound.

CRANE SINKING
DOWN INTO THE KUA

CRANE EXPANDING
CHI TO BOTH SIDES

7. It is very important that you synchronize these three movements. When you do this you will feel the Chi pressure increasing in the abdomen, the lower Tan Tien, and the palms of your hands. The kua and the hip joints will open more due to this Chi pressure.

8. Repeat several times. Complete the exercise with the ending practice discussed at the end of this chapter.

Bear

This animal posture works with the back part of the lower Tan Tien, the sacrum, and the whole back.

1. Begin in the basic standing posture.
2. Inhale, pulling up the anus and perineum, simultaneously making the high-pitched dragon sound. Feel the vacuum sensation in the lower abdomen and the throat sucking Chi into and expanding the lower abdomen and the throat.
3. At the same time, raise the hands up to the heavens to scoop up the Chi and pour it down.
4. Exhale quickly with the low, growling tiger sound.
5. At the same time, pull the back part of the anus up even more. Sink down a little in the kua.

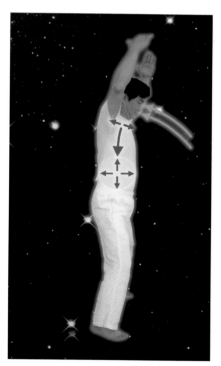 

BEAR POSTURE: INHALE AND EXHALE

6. Press the hands down near the hips. Turn the arms so the fingers point inward. Screw and twist the ulna and radius bones in opposite directions (see figure opposite, top right). Feel the two bones crossing each other. Feel the whole arm and scapula become one piece. As the arm turns and the fingers point inward, the scapulae will be pulled out and the upper back will round.

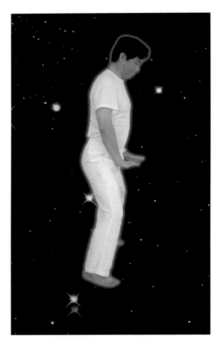

BEAR PRESSES THE HANDS DOWN

7. At the same time, twist the ankles and the knees so that the two bones cross each other (see figure opposite, bottom left). This will make the whole leg be one piece.

8. Twist the heels slightly out and the toes slightly in. The secret is to turn the bones "in but not in, out but not out." This will create a strong balance. Feel the hips and sacrum open, the chest sink, and the scapulae round. The Chi will fill the whole back. While rounding the shoulders, you will feel the whole back expanding like a bear.

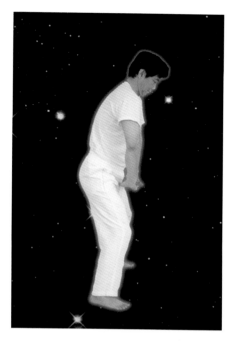

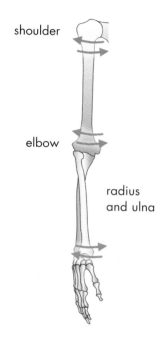

shoulder

elbow

radius
and ulna

BEAR TWISTS ARMS

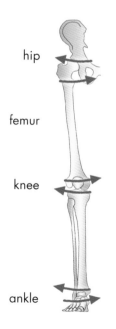

hip

femur

knee

ankle

BEAR TWISTS LEGS

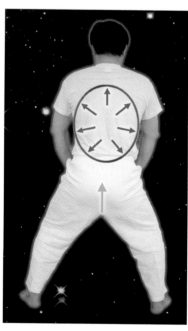

BEAR ROUNDS AND EXPANDS THE BACK

9. Inhale and exhale with the dragon and tiger breaths. Inhale once more with the dragon breath and hold the breath. Tighten and "seal" the neck and the anus so the whole torso feels like a vacuum pack than cannot leak. Suck in and suck out without breathing the air in, and feel the pressure increase in the whole torso. This will increase the circulation of blood, Chi, and lymphatic fluids, and will massage all the organs. Exhale and relax for a while.

10. Now inhale, turn the palms out and up, and raise your palms up, facing the heavens, and scoop up the Chi and pour it down. Lower the hands down to the navel, cover the navel for a while, and feel the warmth.

11. Complete the exercise with the ending practice discussed at the end of this chapter.

 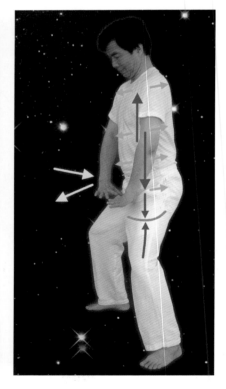

BEAR POSTURE: LEGS SCREWED IN, KUA OPEN, ARMS ONE PIECE WITH SCAPULAE AND SPINE, BACK EXPANDED

BEAR POSTURE: SIDE VIEW

Swallow

This exercise develops Chi pressure on the left and right sides of the lower Tan Tien.

1. Begin in the basic standing posture.
2. Move into the "embrace the tree" position: arms rounded, chest sunk (see figure below left).
3. Inhale, pulling up the anus and perineum, simultaneously making the high-pitched dragon sound. Feel the vacuum sensation in the lower abdomen and the throat sucking Chi into and expanding the lower abdomen and the throat. Exhale with the low, growling tiger sound.

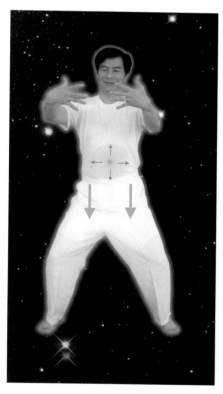
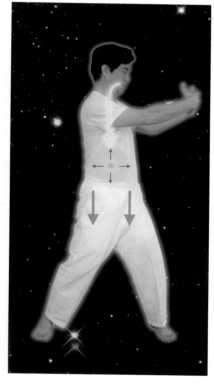

SWALLOW EMBRACES THE TREE   SWALLOW MOVES TO THE LEFT

4. Now, let the Chi in the lower Tan Tien pull you to the left from the lower lumbar (see figure on preceding page, lower right). Feel the Chi pressure.

5. Inhale, pulling up the anus and perineum. Feel the vacuum sensation in the lower abdomen and the throat sucking Chi into and expanding the lower abdomen and the throat.

6. Push the Chi down into the left side and keep the anus lightly contracted.

7. Sink down a little from the groin and feel your left leg pushing down into the earth. Feel a force coming up from the earth and a force pushing you down.

8. Continue with the dragon and tiger breaths and expand the pressure in the lower Tan Tien. Hold this position for a while.

9. Now, let the Chi in the lower Tan Tien pull you back to the middle from the lower lumbar (see figure below). Feel the Chi pressure.

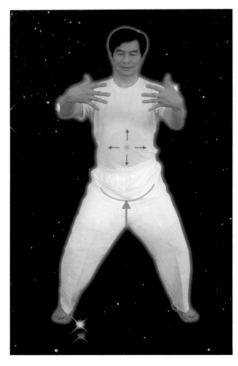

SWALLOW MOVES BACK TO THE MIDDLE

10. Inhale, pulling up the anus and perineum. Feel the vacuum sensation in the lower abdomen and the throat sucking Chi into and expanding the lower abdomen and the throat.

11. Push the Chi down into the middle of the abdomen and keep the anus lightly contracted.

12. Sink down a little from the groin and feel both legs pushing down into the earth. Feel a force coming up from the earth and a force pushing you down.

13. Continue with the dragon and tiger breaths and expand the pressure in the lower Tan Tien. Hold this position for a while.

14. Now, let the Chi in the lower Tan Tien pull you to the right from the lower lumbar (see figure below). Feel the Chi pressure.

15. Inhale, pulling up the anus and perineum. Feel the vacuum sensation in the lower abdomen and the throat sucking Chi into and expanding the lower abdomen and the throat.

sink kua down

SWALLOW MOVES TO THE RIGHT

16. Push the Chi down into the right side and keep the anus lightly contracted.
17. Sink down a little from the groin and feel the right leg pushing down into the earth. Feel a force coming up from the earth and a force pushing you down.
18. Continue with the dragon and tiger breaths and expand the pressure in the lower Tan Tien. Hold this position for a while.
19. Let the Chi in the lower Tan Tien pull you back to the center embracing the tree position.
20. Complete the exercise with the ending practice discussed at the end of this chapter.

Dragon

This exercise develops Chi pressure on the left and right sides of the lower Tan Tien.

DRAGON FACING FRONT

1. Begin in the basic standing posture. Bring the fists to hip level (see figure on preceding page).
2. Inhale, pulling up the anus and perineum, simultaneously making the high-pitched dragon sound. Feel the vacuum sensation in the lower abdomen and the throat sucking Chi into and expanding the lower abdomen and the throat. Exhale with the low, growling tiger sound.
3. Now, let the Chi in the lower Tan Tien pull you to the left from the lower lumbar (see figure below). Feel the Chi pressure.
4. Push the Chi down into the left side and keep the anus lightly contracted.

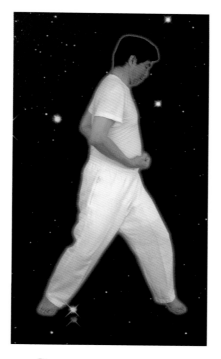

DRAGON MOVES TO THE LEFT

5. Continue with the dragon and tiger breaths and expand the pressure in the lower Tan Tien. Hold this position for a while.

6. Then exhale with the tiger sound quickly, lightly pulling up the left side of the anus. At the same time thrust the right fist down along the left leg to the ground.

7. Feel the left side of the lower Tan Tien expanding.

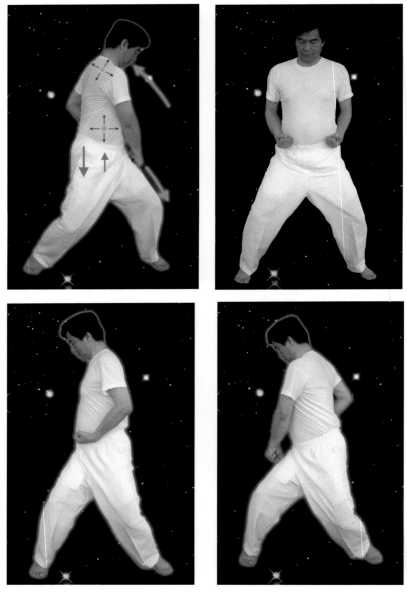

DRAGON THRUSTS FIST DOWN TO THE EARTH, LEFT AND RIGHT

8. Now, let the Chi in the lower Tan Tien pull you back to the middle from the lower lumbar. Feel the Chi pressure.

9. Push the Chi down into the lower abdomen and keep the anus lightly contracted.

10. Continue with the dragon and tiger breaths and expand the pressure in the lower Tan Tien. Hold this position for a while.

11. Then exhale with the tiger sound quickly, lightly pulling up on the middle part of the anus. At the same time thrust both fists straight down (see figure below).

12. Feel the entire lower Tan Tien expanding.

13. Now, let the Chi in the lower Tan Tien pull you to the right from the lower lumbar. Feel the Chi pressure.

14. Push the Chi down into the right side and keep the anus lightly contracted.

15. Continue with the dragon and tiger breaths and expand the pressure in the lower Tan Tien. Hold this position for a while.

DRAGON THRUSTS FIST DOWN TO THE EARTH, CENTER

16. Then exhale with the tiger sound quickly, lightly pulling up the right side of the anus. At the same time thrust the left fist down along the right leg to the ground.
17. Feel the right side of the lower Tan Tien expanding.
18. Complete the exercise with the ending practice explained at the end of this chapter.

Eagle

This exercise develops Chi pressure throughout the lower Tan Tien.

1. Begin in the basic standing posture.
2. Inhale, pulling up the anus and perineum, simultaneously making the high-pitched dragon sound. Feel the vacuum sensation in the lower abdomen and the throat sucking Chi into and expanding the lower abdomen and the throat.

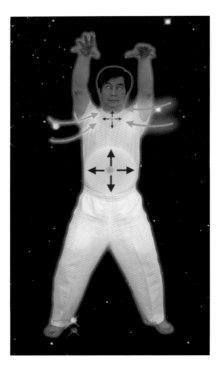

EAGLE FLIES

3. At the same time, raise the arms above the head, with the elbows slightly bent and the fingers spread out. Roll your eyes up and fix them on the crown.

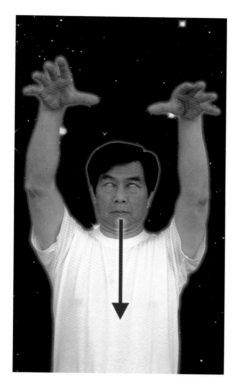

EAGLE ROLLS EYES TO THE CROWN

4. Exhale quickly with the low, growling tiger sound.
5. Pull up the anus up even more and press the Chi down into the lower Tan Tien.
6. Just stand in this position, repeating the dragon and tiger breaths.
7. Repeat three to six times. This exercise will enhance the Chi in the lower Tan Tien and in your fingers.
8. Complete the exercise with the ending practice discussed at the end of this chapter.

Monkey

This exercise develops Chi pressure in the whole lower Tan Tien area.

1. Begin in the basic standing posture. Place your palms in front of the kua.
2. Inhale, pulling up the anus and perineum, simultaneously making the high-pitched dragon sound. Feel the vacuum sensation in the lower abdomen and the throat sucking Chi into and expanding the lower abdomen and the throat.
3. At the same time, raise the arms above the head with the palms open.
4. Exhale quickly with the low, growling tiger sound.

MONKEY RAISES ARMS

5. At the same time, squat down from the kua.
6. Push the Chi pressure down into the lower Tan Tien with the sound.
7. Swing both arms to the ground.

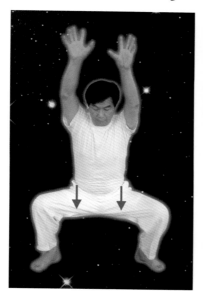

MONKEY SQUATS

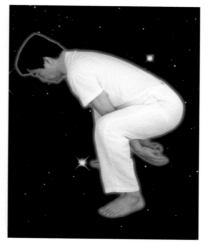

MONKEY GATHERS EARTH CHI

8. Continue swinging both arms up and down while squatting like a monkey. In this exercise, the upper part of your body is light while the lower part is heavy. Feel the kua open more. Gather the earth Chi into the palms and bones.

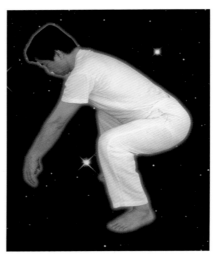

MONKEY SWINGING ARMS

MONKEY RISES, BRINGING EARTH CHI UP

9. Inhale, rising up from the hips, returning to the starting position.
10. Open your palms to absorb the heavenly Chi.
11. Repeat these steps three to six times. Finish with the ending exercise at the end of this chapter.

MONKEY ABSORBS HEAVENLY CHI

Elephant

This exercise develops Chi pressure on the left and right sides of the lower Tan Tien.

1. Begin in the basic standing posture.
2. Inhale, pulling up the anus and perineum, simultaneously making the high-pitched dragon sound. Feel the vacuum sensation in the lower abdomen and the throat sucking Chi into and expanding the lower abdomen and the throat.

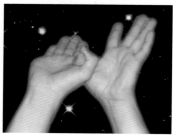

ELEPHANT RAISES TRUNK

3. At the same time, hook the thumbs together and raise your arms above your head.
4. Turn your hips to the left side.
5. Exhale with the tiger sound and press the Chi down to the lower Tan Tien. Pull up the anus and the left tide of the anus.
6. Now turn your hips to the center and swing your arms, like the trunk of an elephant, down to the ground. Swing the arms like a trunk back and forth to gather the earth Chi.

ELEPHANT SWINGS TRUNK, GATHERING EARTH CHI

7. Inhale with dragon sound as you gradually rise up. The palms scoop up the earth energy. Come back up to the starting position, with the arms raised above the crown. Turn the hips to the right side.

ELEPHANT RAISES TRUNK FROM THE EARTH TO THE HEAVENS

8. Exhale with the tiger sound and press the Chi down to the lower Tan Tien. Pull up the anus and the left side of the anus.
9. Turn your hips to the center and swing your arms, like the trunk of an elephant, down to the ground. Swing the arms like a trunk back and forth to gather the earth Chi.
10. Repeat the whole exercise three times.
11. Rest and do the ending exercise described at the end of this chapter.

Rhinoceros

This exercise develops Chi pressure on the left and right sides of the lower Tan Tien.

1. Begin in the basic standing posture.
2. Inhale, pulling up the anus and perineum, simultaneously making the high-pitched dragon sound. Feel the vacuum sensation in the lower abdomen and the throat sucking Chi into and expanding the lower abdomen and the throat.
3. At the same time, step your left foot in front of your right foot, and place your right foot at a forty-five degree angle behind you.
4. Stretch your left arm out straight in front of you, the palm facing downward. Hold the back of your right hand in front of your forehead.
5. Inhale with the dragon sound. Pull up the anus and the left side of the anus, and sink a little bit in the kua.

RHINOCEROS STRETCHES ARM OUT   RHINOCEROS SIDE VIEW

6. Now, move the waist with the lower Tan Tien to the left. Your hips and navel should stay pointed straight in front of you. The arms and the upper body move to the left.

7. Exhale with the tiger sound. Pull up the left side of the anus more and, at the same time, press the Chi down into the left side of the lower Tan Tien. Press the left leg into the ground.

8. Hold this position and continue the dragon and tiger breaths. Build up the inner abdominal pressure.

9. When out of breath, exhale and inhale. Regulate the breath; rest.

10. Repeat on the right side, the right leg in front and the left leg at a forty-five degree angle behind you. Stretch the right arm straight out in front of you and hold the back of the left hand in front of your forehead.

11. Inhale with the dragon sound. Pull up the anus and the right side of the anus. Sink a little bit in the kua. Turn the waist with the lower Tan Tien to the right. The navel and hips should not move.

RHINOCEROS MOVES TO THE RIGHT

12. Exhale with the tiger sound. Pull up the right side of the anus more and, at the same time, press the Chi down into the right side of the lower Tan Tien. Press your right leg in the ground.

13. Hold this position and continue the dragon and tiger breaths. Build up the inner abdominal pressure.

14. When out of breath, exhale and inhale. Regulate the breath; rest.

15. Do the ending exercise at the end of this chapter.

Horse

This exercise develops Chi pressure in the solar plexus.

1. Begin in the basic standing posture.

2. Inhale, pulling up the anus and perineum, simultaneously making the high-pitched dragon sound. Feel the vacuum sensation in the lower abdomen and the throat sucking Chi into and expanding the lower abdomen and the throat.

HORSE POSTURE BEGINS

3. At the same time, raise the arms above the head, and, while inhaling, suck in the upper abdomen toward the back. Flatten the navel area so that the navel touches the spine.

4. Sink a little in the kua and at the same time exhale quickly, with force, and press the arms down with force, especially the wrists.

5. At the same time, push the abdomen out with the horse sound (*Ho*). It is an echo sound coming from the solar plexus.

6. Do the horse sound with the arm movement three to six times. Rest.

7. Do the ending exercise explained at the end of this chapter.

HORSE EXHALES *"HO,"* PRESSING DOWN WITH THE ARMS AND WRISTS

Bull

This exercise develops Chi pressure in the back part of the lower Tan Tien. From this exercise you will learn to sink back in the kua, move from the Tan Tien with the Tan Tien force, and direct the force through the spine to the fingertips and from the fingertips back into the earth.

1. Begin in the basic standing posture.
2. Inhale, pulling up the anus and perineum, simultaneously making the high-pitched dragon sound. Feel the vacuum sensation in the lower abdomen and the throat sucking Chi into and expanding the lower abdomen and the throat.
3. At the same time, step your right foot in front of your left foot, and place your left foot at a forty-five degree angle behind you.
4. Stretch your arms out straight in front of you, the palms facing downward.

BULL STRETCHES ARMS OUT

5. Inhale, pulling up on the anus. Sink down a little in the kua.

6. Turn the palms and scoop up the Chi on the left and right sides. Press down into both legs.

7. Now, spiral the hands with the tendons under the armpits until the palms are facing you. "Find the straight in the curve," which means that when you twist the wrist and the elbow, hold the twist and try to straighten the arms, creating a force in the arms.

BULL SCOOPS UP THE CHI

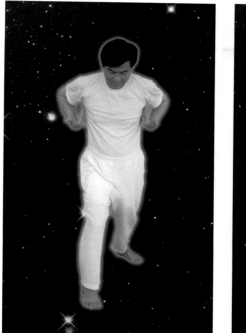

"FIND THE STRAIGHT IN THE CURVE"

8. Exhale with the tiger sound and press the Chi down to the lower abdomen. At the same time pull up the front side of the anus.

9. Spiral the hands more until the palms are facing outward, and push the hands out in front of you. Push the energy out into the fingertips.

10. At the same time, let the Chi in the lower Tan Tien push down into both legs.

11. Feel the energy rising from the earth. Pull up the front and back side of the anus.

12. Round the sacrum/lower back, with your chest in, scapulae round, and chin pushed back. Feel the energy rising in the spine.

13. Repeat the whole sequence three to six times in this position, then rest.

14. Alternate sides, with the left leg in front and the right leg back.

Repeat the whole sequence three to six times in this position, then rest.

15. Complete with the ending exercise at the end of this chapter.

WITH THE TIGER BREATH, BULL PUSHES THE CHI OUT TO THE FRONT

ENDING EXERCISE FOR ANIMAL POSTURES

After each animal exercise, perform the following steps to energize the whole body and collect the Chi in the lower Tan Tien.

1. Stand with feet together. Inhale and scoop up the energy from the universe, palms facing up.
2. Now, turn the palms downward and pour the energy down over the body, back into the navel, back into the lower Tan Tien.

PALMS OPENED UPWARD

POUR THE CHI DOWN

3. Focus on the door of life (located between the third and forth lumbar vertebrae, just beneath the two kidneys, and opposite the navel). Gently, move the hands from the navel to the thighs.

Feel the fingers and Chi penetrate the thighbones as Chi is absorbed into the bone marrow.

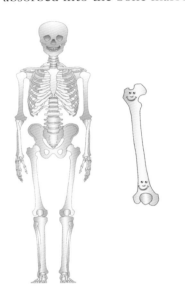 

TOUCH THE THIGHBONES

4. Bending over, move the hands down the thighbones. Feel the fingers penetrate the bones, glide past the knees, and across the shinbones.

MOVE THE FINGERS DOWN THE LEGS

5. Now, as you glide the hands down, sink the hips and bring the tailbone down to the heels in a squatting position.

SQUAT DOWN

6. Feel yourself sinking down through the earth and into the infinite space beyond the earth. Picture the galaxy and feel the spiraling of the universal energy.

7. With your hands touching your feet, lift the tailbone until the legs are straight. Feel the Chi drawn from outer space and the earth spiraling into your body.

LIFT THE TAILBONE

8. Squat down again and gather more earth energy and more universal energy. Repeat this three to nine times.

9. Move your fingers to the back of the shinbones. Feel the fingers touch the heel bones and press into the bone marrow.

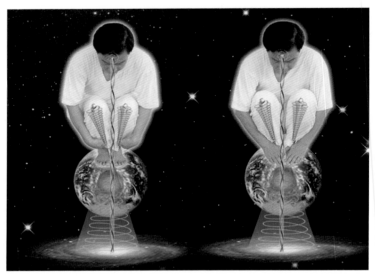

SQUAT DOWN AGAIN

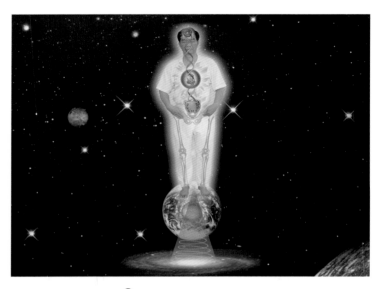

GLIDE FINGERS UP TO HIPS

10. Now, glide the fingers up the leg bones to the hips. Then bring the fingers to the coccyx and hold them there for a while. Feel the Chi rising to the spine and the brain.

11. Move the fingers to the sacrum. Feel the Chi pour into the sacrum and the sexual center.

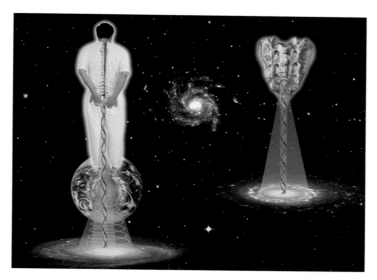

TOUCH THE COCCYX AND SACRUM

FEEL THE CHI POUR INTO THE SPINE

12. Bring the hands up to the door of life and concentrate on the navel. Feel the Chi energizing the kidneys and the door of life.

13. Slowly bring the hands to the navel. Visualize all the energy you have generated through your practices condensing and spiraling into the lower Tan Tien, where it will be safely stored. Smile and feel the Chi vibrating in the lower Tan Tien. Breathe in a slow, deep, relaxed manner. Rest.

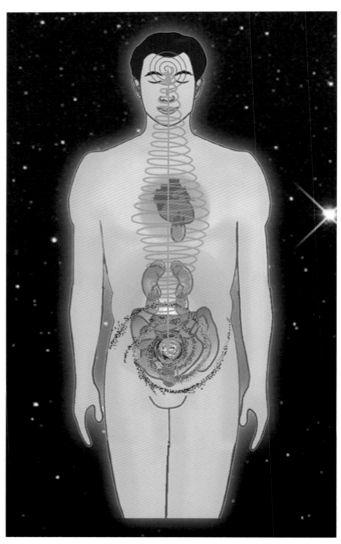

COLLECT THE CHI IN THE LOWER TAN TIEN

Chi Kung, Health, and Healing

THE BODY'S WISDOM

In order to create and preserve internal pressure and Chi power in the lower Tan Tien, it is essential that we turn inward and begin to listen to our body and its natural wisdom. We need to learn to understand and interpret its signs and processes.

As a rule, various "sediments" accumulate in our organs and glands from early traumas that we have not been able or willing to give up. We may even have cherished them, as they give us reason to continue living in a state of separation and depression, so that we can justify our state of "dis-ease" and negative emotions.

Disease may be a sign calling upon us to awaken, and an invitation to turn inward. The vision and theory that inspires Tan Tien Chi Kung and that lies at the very root of Chinese medicine is that health is the natural outcome of self-reliance and the assumption of responsibility for one's own life, attitudes, and conduct. The practices of Tan Tien Chi Kung can help us to become aware of energy patterns in our bodies, and to work through blockages.

Unlike the Western approach to health and medicine, Chi Kung does not focus on particular parts of the body when sickness or pain are experienced. It looks at the totality of the processes taking place in the relations between the five elements and phases, so that imbalances are holistically treated.

Chi Kung is based on premises that are qualitatively different from those inspiring modern Western conceptions of medicine. It is a process and method to increase Chi pressure to enhance health, self-healing, and energy transformation.

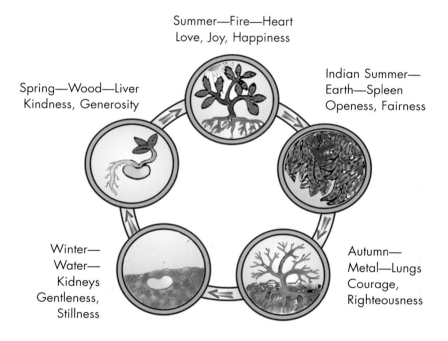

BALANCING THE FIVE ELEMENTS AND PHASES

SUBTLE WONDERS

Subtle wonders lie in the small spaces of awareness that arise every day. Subtle wonders may arise at any time under any circumstance as moments of awakening to our inner powers and potentials. In these moments of awareness, we may be awakened to the Chi Kung state, a meditative state that can also be called "entering silence." In the Chi Kung state, we can tap energy from the cosmos.

Subtle wonders arise from the deep-down longing for infinity, from which a sense of curiosity arises. In this curiosity there is an open-mindedness that enables us to see reality from a new angle. Our energy changes and we begin to feel and see ourselves and the world in a new way.

Chi Kung, and especially Tan Tien Chi Kung, through all the exercises of grounding and centering, can help in reconnecting with ourselves, the earth, and the universe. A sense of belonging arises in our body, as well as a sense of the unity and interconnectedness of all phenomena. Humility is a state of being truthful and sensitive to this insight.

To the extent that we are able to forgive and accept ourselves, others, and the world, we create an ability in ourselves to return to our prenatal breathing pattern, and not only create peace within ourselves but also around us. Such an attitude will help us to view problems not as obstacles but as opportunities for learning and solving them "from within." It is significant in this context that the Chinese word for "crisis" has at the same time a negative as well as a positive connotation. What is a problem, a "negative" occurrence, is at the same time an opportunity to learn.

This is precisely the deep sense of the yin and yang symbol, in which there is a light spot in the dark and a dark spot in the light. This insight honors the inherent reality of the unity of opposites in everything in the universe, including ourselves.

YIN AND YANG SYMBOL

All genuine transformations invariably start as small awakenings, subtle wonders that were hardly perceptible. We may experience some of these subtle wonders as we begin to practice Tan Tien Chi Kung. For example, one subtle wonder is the discovery of the ability to differentiate and activate the different points of the anus. You learn to coordinate the contraction of the anus and the perineum so as to seal the pelvic floor. This creates internal pressure through the creation of the Chi ball, and this opens the way for self-reliance, self-healing, and self-realization.

Another subtle wonder is the discovery of the numerous benefits that arise from the squatting practices. We feel the opening of the kua, which makes us more grounded and lighter at the same time. We find that we can walk straight and tall, and see the world with new eyes.

CHI KUNG AS ACTIVE ENERGY MEDITATION

Chinese Taoist practice took a different approach from spiritual paths that emphasized a separation between body and mind. In some of these traditions, "mortification" of the body was practiced, as well as forms of meditation in which the mind is disconnected from the body. The Taoist approach emerged because it was observed that some of these traditions led to a serious contempt for the body, thereby undermining balance, ease, and well-being.

The Taoist approach focuses on the integration of mind with Chi and the cultivation and transformation of Chi as an internal active meditation. In this it is different from all other approaches to meditation. Undoubtedly this Chinese innovation is deeply connected with the pragmatic sense of life that is so characteristic of Chinese culture. At the same time, with its emphasis on the integration of action and contemplation, Taoist practice has had a pervasive influence on the flowering of Chinese civilization in all fields, particularly science, medicine, and the arts.

The Taoist, active approach to meditation has its roots in a positive relationship to the entire body and in particular to sexuality. Sexuality is, in most religious traditions and "high" cultures (in contrast to indigenous and folk cultures), treated with contempt and fear, as it is associated with the "lower" part of the body. It is seen as the locus of animal instincts and therefore an obstacle to "higher" pursuits.

The practice of Chi Kung enables people to take care of themselves—body, mind, soul, and spirit—and make use of their own innate potential to cultivate total health, growth, and transformation. In the process of Chi Kung practice, new forms of consciousness/spirit arise that we are able to direct for the healing and well being of ourselves, others, and the environment around us.

SELF-HEALING AND WHOLENESS

In the Taoist tradition, the lower body and its organs and functions are associated with the earth, and the upper body and its organs and functions are associated with heaven. Yet the spiritual body cannot be born and grow without being nourished by an unceasing supply of fresh Chi, generated in the lower body by the practice of Tan Tien Chi Kung.

Tan Tien Chi Kung, as one of the basic practices of the Taoist approach to health and self-healing, has its roots in a particular worldview that is at the very heart of Chinese civilization and science. In this view, human beings, like all other creatures, are seen as part of nature.

Human beings are not above and on top of nature, but need to serve and honor it. Nature is not to be conquered but to be treated with reverence and respect. People have to live in harmony with the universe and with nature as its manifestation. If not, the universe will turn against humans beings and destroy the very foundations of their lives.

In this ancient Taoist vision, at the heart of Chi Kung and Tan Tien Chi Kung, the universe and the earth are seen and experienced

TAN TIEN CHI KUNG

as sacred. Also, the human body is seen as a sacred vessel and a micro-cosmos in which the macrocosmos is mirrored and reproduced.

In the same vein, all that exists is holy, and life is seen as a process of return to the original state of holiness/wholeness in which the primordial unity with the universe is regained. Healing, wholeness, and holiness have the same etymological root.

Heaven and earth, dark and light, the sacred and the profane, the material and the spiritual, body and mind, the physical and the metaphysical, thinking and feeling, what is above and what is below, are not seen as irreconcilable or inimical opposites but as natural polarities and partners between yin and yang. This manifests the relations between heaven/fire and earth/water, at the root of the energetic processes of imbalance and balance within the body.

The lower Tan Tien is not a physical phenomenon but an energy field of the subtle body. It has therefore not a precise physical location but varies with each person, depending on sex, age, and life history. It functions in the area just between the navel, the door of life, and the sexual center, just above the pelvic area.

In view of the above, Tan Tien Chi Kung may be defined as an energy meditation or inner fitness practice, designed to enhance a Chi Kung state of being in ourselves by awakening, activating, and sustaining processes, rhythms, flows, and transformations of energy in the body.

As discussed throughout this book, the lower Tan Tien is the center of activation and balancing of the Chi in the body. Tan Tien Chi Kung, like other forms of Chi Kung, is not only a source of self-healing but may also serve as a source of healing others. However, its effectiveness depends on the energy of the healer. To practice healing others by way of Chi Kung, healers need first to raise their own energy, so that they can share their abundance.

Through the practice of Chi Kung, a high energy field is created that may then serve to activate the energy fields of those who seek to be healed. If the person who seeks healing were to have a higher energy field, it may well be that the healer would drain that person. Thus for any healer, the first responsibility lies in healing themselves so that their work will be a blessing. For this reason, energy meditations are the first responsibility of the Taoist practitioner who intends to be a healer. To raise energies, Chi pressure is indispensable. While an abundant Chi supply is essential for health, inversely, good health is also a condition for an abundant Chi supply.

Thus, to ensure both physical health and spiritual growth, an abundant supply of Chi is needed. This accumulation of Chi is

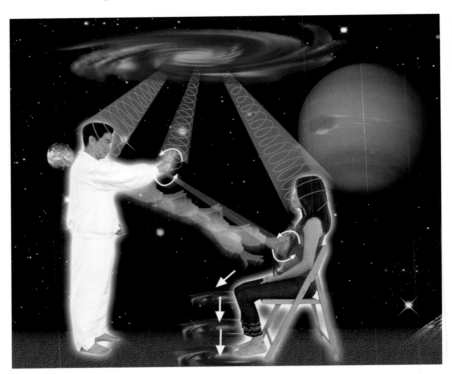

COSMIC HEALING

indispensable for creating the right kind of pressure to sustain and enhance the free and optimal flow of energy throughout the whole body. Chi is needed to activate the blood and lymph flows, the flow of the cerebrospinal fluids, the nerves, the endocrine glands and hormones, the fascia, and the tendons, bones, muscles and all the cells of the body.

As an electromagnetic force, Chi is the source of all movement and power in the universe. It is also the source of life and empowerment of the whole body and all its functions. It can only be properly used and serve body and spirit if it is activated, guided, and directed by the mind.

CONSCIOUSNESS AND RELAXATION

In recent brain research, it has been found that the average person uses only four to five percent of his or her brain cells. This small portion of active brain cells lies at the surface of the cerebrum. It means that the vast numbers of brain cells in the deeper layers of the cerebrum are asleep.

It is difficult for these cells to be activated if one is too stressed and overactive. Our competitive modern cultures make stress and tension an essential condition for "keeping up." Such stress makes it difficult to nourish and maintain Chi pressure.

Chi Kung serves to create a state of relaxation that enables the practitioner to return to his or "natural state." Then the deeper layers of the brain can be opened up and the creative powers of the unconsciousness mind, where all originality and creativity lie hidden, become available. Chi Kung practice can serve to significantly activate dormant electromagnetic currents in the deep brain and thereby bring about a major change in the nature of awareness.

Relaxation is not static. Rather, it is an expression of the dynamic balance that comes about when one is aligned with the force of gravity. We experience the pulls of the opposite forces within ourselves: the force that pulls up, the force that pulls down, and the various forces from the electrical and magnetic fields in the universe. Chi Kung is the art of being in balance with all these forces through the process of mutual adjustment of body, mind, and breathing. Our posture facilitates this balance as internal pressure and power are generated.

The ability of the lower Tan Tien to activate Chi significantly depends on the degree to which the chest diaphragm retains (or regains) its flexibility and becomes relaxed so that it can freely move up and down. The chest diaphragm has a pumping function that can exert pressure on the lower Tan Tien through practices that pack and release Chi. (The perineum power practices, discussed in Chapter 7, rely on this action of the chest diaphragm.) Chi pressure is raised and condensed through the packing process.

Through the practice of packing and releasing, the whole lower Tan Tien receives a massage. This activates the organs and expels toxins and sediments from the organs in the abdomen, so that blood and Chi flow are restored.

The small and large intestines also share in the benefits of this packing process, as they are massaged and the natural peristaltic movement is reactivated. It is well known that many chronic diseases originate in the bowels. The Tan Tien Chi Kung exercises designed to open the kua work on pressing the bowel into proper movement.

REACTIVATION AND REGENERATION

The activation of the abdomen plays a major role in the creation of a state of ease and the prevention of "dis-ease." If the abdomen is at ease, the whole body comes to rest. If not, the whole body suffers, as the basic metabolism is affected. In the process of aging and as a result of an agitated lifestyle, the abdominal organs tend to sag and thereby lose their vitality. These organs, thanks to the rise in Chi pressure in the lower Tan Tien, can be uplifted and brought back in their original position, so that once again the Chi flows.

After giving birth, the uterus may sag and interfere with the proper functioning of the transverse colon. If undue pressure is placed on the fallopian tubes and the ovaries, proper blood and Chi flow is prevented and toxins cannot be moved out. This in turn may lead to serious diseases. Thus, women can receive particular benefit from Tan Tien Chi Kung.

The chest diaphragm can move down if the lower Tan Tien is freed from mental and emotional stress and tension. This is a principal cause of constipation and degeneration of the digestive and eliminative system. Constipation can also be relieved by the lengthening the psoas muscles.

By generating Chi in the lower Tan Tien, we dissolve tensions in the body, and bring down and cool excess fire energy, which always rises up and tends to overheat the brain, heart, and lungs. This cools the body, reestablishing the natural balance between fire and water energies.

By concentrating attention on the lower Tan Tien, we also bring down the point of gravity in the body so that stability increases and the earth connection is enhanced. As we become more rooted, a sense of coming home may arise. This has a further cooling and refreshing effect on the body.

With the downward movement of the chest diaphragm, the lungs also get new space. They have suffered from the stress and tension that has caused breathing to become short and shallow. When the lower Tan Tien enters a state of ease and the chest diaphragm is able to relax and returns to its natural rhythmic up-and-down movement, the lungs can ease into their natural function.

Then one can start again to breath deeply, slowly, and gently. This regenerates the whole body, as its cells, organs, glands, and bones become toned and energized as a consequence of the fresh Chi pressure. Nose breathing becomes less necessary and can gradually give way to breathing from within.

As a result of this process toward inner relaxation and balance, the body can start to function in a qualitatively new way; it needs to rely less on external air intake and more on the Chi from within, the original or prenatal Chi. Breathing becomes again a natural rhythmic process that occurs by itself and that creates the right pressure needed for the body to function optimally.

The reactivation and regeneration of the body, and the emergence of new consciousness, is indeed a real possibility. But it does not come about by itself; it requires continuous exercise and practice that is light and playful, as if it were a child's game.

Chi and the Tao

THE LOWER TAN TIEN AND CHI KUNG

The lower Tan Tien is where the energy condensation process that begins our life occurs. This is where all the energies of heaven and earth and the essences of our parents and ancestors come together and create the embryo and our original Chi. The birth of the very universe from nothingness is reflected in the beginning of our life journey in the lower Tan Tien.

By smiling and relaxing into the belly, we ease the metabolism in the whole body, facilitating the digestion of food and creating favorable conditions for the greater digestive process: the processing and blending of universal, earth, and cosmic Chi to support the growth of the embryo.

By focusing our loving attention on the lower Tan Tien, we create the primary conditions for regeneration and rejuvenation. When we grow older, we also can grow younger, as we remember our original prenatal state, cultivate our inner power, and develop and maintain Chi pressure.

The cosmic inner smile (discussed in Chapter 3) is the foundation of Tan Tien Chi Kung as an active energy meditation. It prepares the ground for all other Universal Tao exercises. The presence of inner peace determines to what extent all the Chi Kung exercises will be effective. The ability to deeply relax is very important in the absorp-

COSMIC INNER SMILE

tion of high-energy substances. These substances are the focus of Chi Kung and its process of transformation.

The lower Tan Tien processes and balances the emotional energies, which have their seat in the organs, and then returns the virtuous energies to them. Subsequently it nourishes the whole body with the blended and refined energies. This process must be supported by fresh energy, which can only come from good Chi pressure.

In the higher alchemical Kan and Li practices (an advanced Universal Tao practice), it is once again the lower Tan Tien that serves as the first station for alchemical transformation. Here the water energy is steamed by the fire energy so that the whole body is cleansed and detoxified and the transformation processes at the higher centers of the heart and the brain are prepared.

For all these alchemical transformations, a high accumulation of concentrated Chi is needed. To supply this Chi, Tan Tien Chi Kung plays a key role. This explains why Taoist Masters and practitioners in their meditations always center on the lower Tan Tien. It is here that the whole bioelectromagnetic process that nourishes and sustains successive waves of electromagnetic activation is set in motion. Maintaining a firm but gentle Chi pressure in the lower Tan Tien is important in all forms of Chi Kung.

Chi Kung requires a form of movement that is exactly counter to that of today's global culture, with its upward movement that disconnects people from the earth so that they lose their structural align-

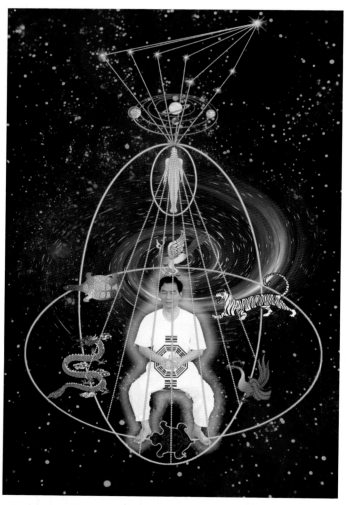

ADVANCED KAN AND LI PRACTICE RELIES ON LOWER TAN TIEN

ment with gravity and their Chi pressure. As a result they lose their inner power, physically, mentally, and spiritually.

When the center of gravity moves down into the lower Tan Tien, one starts to feel lighter; it is as if one is less affected by the law of gravity and feels more free and spacious as well as more grounded. This opens the way for the transfer of consciousness into higher bodies that are free of gravity.

This is only safe and wise, in the Taoist view, if and when the body remains grounded and centered. The higher you want to go, the more you have to be grounded. Chi pressure in the lower Tan Tien is essential for this grounding. One can push Chi pressure downward into the ground, so that the earth force will resonate and bounce up in the opposite direction.

If one is not grounded and centered and there is no good Chi pressure in the lower Tan Tien, fear tends to accumulate, and then it will be even more difficult to become centered and grounded. Fear blocks the free flow of Chi by creating tension in the body, especially in the kidneys.

When one is not grounded, the connection with the earth declines and the sense of being at ease in one's own body is weakened. Life is increasingly experienced in terms of outside pressure. This leads to an inner state in which the body feels compelled to experience life as a threat coming from outside against which the body has to defend itself.

In this process the body's energies, rather than serving the growth of inner balance, are turned against "the others" and the world as the actual or potential enemy. The very basis of existence becomes one that is marked by and legitimizes aggression. Competition and the creation of a win/lose situation becomes a compulsion.

In this situation, Tan Tien Chi Kung and other Taoist practices are a blessing, as they help the student to rediscover and regain the inner way of reconnecting with their own center and ground. They also create awareness of the inner structure of the body and of the glorious unity between high and low, heaven and earth, and the mutual relationships between the sexual organs, the perineum, the anus, the belly, the mind, and the spirit.

When grounded and rooted, one can come to feel at home and at ease and peace with oneself. Then one becomes less vulnerable and swayed by the external circumstances, no matter what happens around one.

The Tan Tien Chi Kung training of smiling to one's pelvic floor and embracing all of one's body functions enables one, both physically and psychologically, to remain centered and rooted. The more you are centered and rooted, the less others can push you.

Training in becoming grounded, moving from your center, and developing perineum power has major implications for one's relationship to the world. If one feels safe and at ease within oneself, there is no need to project one's own negative energies on others. As a result, others are less likely to see you as their opponent or enemy. Also, as one exudes inner power, there is reason for others to be respectful.

The more intimate you become with the energies of the universe in your inner structure, the less vulnerable you become. That means that you are one with the Tao, and that all imbalances in the pressure from inside and outside have been dissolved.

Chi Kung practice is also a powerful antidote against aging, which is greatly accelerated by a movement upward of the center of gravity, with the consequent loss of power and stability. This movement can be reversed by bringing the focus of attention down to the lower Tan Tien, as occurs in Tan Tien Chi Kung.

For this, the mind has to release all that prevents inner relaxation, as true attention and mindfulness can only grow if the mind is freed from negative emotions and mental states and learns to practice emptiness. Then it can create the conditions for new fullness. One sees that life consists of cycles: fullness and emptiness, living and dying, beginnings and ends, old and new, seasons and phases, days and nights, mornings and evenings, and dark and light. The practice of the various forms of Chi Kung facilitates a continuous flow and balance between the yin and yang and all the cycles of life. We discover that fullness can only arise out of emptiness.

With the center in the lower Tan Tien, the body can move in perfect alignment with gravity. It can only do so if the breath is kept low and the chest diaphragm finds itself in a relaxed state, as it responds to the relaxation in the lower Tan Tien. Such a process toward relaxation is the very aim and art of Tan Tien Chi Kung, which should be practiced as a play of movements; one becomes a child again, finding joy and delight in the practice for its own sake.

WISDOM MIND

Tan Tien Chi Kung involves the simultaneous training of body and mind by way of activating mind power. The combined and integrated activity of the mind, body, breath, and Chi are the major sources of activation of the subtle energy transformations.

The more the mind is awakened, the more the heart is opened, and the more the eye is trained to look inward, the easier it becomes for the mind to lead and guide the movement of Chi through the body. Thus the process of transformation is determined by the progressive refinement and combination of mind, heart, and inner eye into one undivided subtle power. This becomes what is known as the *Yi,* the "one mind" or "wisdom mind."

While the lower Tan Tien serves as the source and the vessel or container of Chi, it is the wisdom mind that leads its movement, distribution, and circulation. The more the wisdom mind is cultivated, the more skillful it will be in sensing where Chi is needed and guide it.

In traditional Chinese teaching, Chi is considered the soldiers and Yi the commander in chief. These martial terms make clear that Chi was of vital importance in the martial arts and in warfare, as it represented the major source of power before gunpowder was introduced. It is not surprising that the ways of access to these powers were kept secret to guard the monopoly and also to avoid abuse.

With the decline of the use of Chi Kung and especially of Iron

WISDOM CHI KUNG

Shirt Chi Kung as a principal weapon in warfare, its yin dimension could be more fully appreciated. Chi Kung gained greater recognition for its utility in healing and spiritual growth.

With the growth of subtle energy through Taoist meditative practice, there is less need to rely on conducting Chi through external practice and effort. The movements increasingly originate from within as both the mind and the body become more sensitive to each

IRON SHIRT CHI KUNG

other and the energies that the body houses become more and more subtle.

However, the overall energy balance in the body always remains the direct outcome of the level of Chi pressure. When Chi pressure decreases, all fluids in the body are deactivated and health declines. When the natural energy balance between fire and water in the body is lost, both body and mind suffer, but especially the brain and the heart.

TAI CHI CHI KUNG

Wisdom relies on listening to and "feeling into" the consciousness of the mind and the whole body and its organs. Knowledge is the accumulation of information and is merely a product of the upper brain. In modern cultures, there is decreasing respect for wisdom. The body and its emotions are seen as a source of disturbance rather than as the "temple of the spirit."

Chi Kung practitioners may correct this imbalance by making more space for water energy and establishing a better connection with the earth energy. The practices of Tan Tien Chi Kung are particularly helpful in this rebalancing, because the lower Tan Tien is the seat of both the water and earth elements.

Tan Tien Chi Kung, Iron Shirt Chi Kung, and Tai Chi Chi Kung, as well as all other Universal Tao practices, are helping practitioners around the world to become rooted and centered and to cultivate the wisdom mind.

CHI KUNG AS SELF-ACTUALIZATION

The ordinary, functioning mind and consciousness cannot maintain a high concentration of Chi. Thus, it behooves us to practice Chi Kung so as to cultivate the wisdom mind and align ourselves with our true nature and the energies of the universe (*Te*).

This is the original meaning of the Chinese character *Te*: human alignment with the whole, the universe. It may also be understood as actualization of the universe or cosmos within oneself, or self-realization. It also carries the connotation of integrity (in its original sense of being undivided), power, and strength. The more one grows toward realizing within oneself this unity with the universe, the higher is one's quality of selfhood, as a microcosmic manifestation of the macrocosmos.

Te suggests a process of alignment "from within." It presupposes independence and self-reliance; one's own mind and body is a field of energy and consciousness and the source of entering into alignment with the Tao. This explains the great sense of independence by Taoist

TE—"ALIGNMENT WITH THE WHOLE"

practitioners and communities over the centuries and their reliance on inner rather than outer authority, knowledge, and power. This sense of independence is conveyed by the legends about the lives of the immortals.

CHAUN CHUNG-LI, ONE OF THE EIGHT IMMORTALS

SURRENDER AND THE CHI KUNG STATE

The practices of Tan Tien Chi Kung are among the many resources the Taoist practitioner uses to connect with the universe. The practice combines the power of the mind with the extension of Chi, which allows our personal consciousness to connect directly to the energy of the earth and universe. Through these practices, we transform Chi into a force that is accessible to us.

Like some other religions and spiritual paths, Taoism places great emphasis on surrender, letting go, and emptiness. This is actually a form of deep relaxation. When we are relaxed, our muscles are open, our breathing is soft, and energy can flow through the channels of our body. There is no resistance and no fighting. This allows the creative and higher forces to flow into us. Through the surrender of control, we open up and touch the forces of nature. However, if we continue to surrender and let go, this energy will drain out of us. To avoid this, we must again become aware of ourselves and our own energy.

The idea that we must surrender while at the same time using our intention, mind, and Chi to draw the energy into ourselves may seem a paradox. However, as we do the practices and learn how to be empty and open and simultaneously draw the force into ourselves, the paradox will resolve itself and we will see the possibilities it enables.

Ultimately, the practice of the Taoist path, of which Chi Kung is a part, leads to the cultivation of the Chi Kung state and the realization of the principle of Wu Wei, or "non-doing." We deeply realize ourselves to be not separate from others and the environment, therefore our actions are not motivated by a sense of separateness. Our actions become spontaneous and effortless, "going with the flow." If we can learn to follow the Tao, practicing "actionless action," then nothing remains undone.

About the Author

Mantak Chia has been studying the Taoist approach to life since childhood. His mastery of this ancient knowledge, enhanced by his study of other disciplines, has resulted in the development of the Universal Tao System, which is now being taught throughout the world.

Mantak Chia was born in Thailand to Chinese parents in 1944. When he was six years old, he learned from Buddhist monks how to sit and "still the mind." While in grammar school he learned traditional Thai boxing, and soon went on to acquire considerable skill in Aikido, Yoga, and Tai Chi. His studies of the Taoist way of life began in earnest when he was a student in Hong Kong, ultimately leading to his mastery of a wide variety of esoteric disciplines. To better understand the mechanisms behind healing energy, he also studied Western anatomy and medical sciences.

Master Chia has taught his system of healing and energizing practices to tens of thousands of students and trained more than two thousand instructors and practitioners throughout the world. He has established centers for Taoist study and training in many countries around the globe. In June 1990 he was honored by the International Congress of Chinese Medicine and Qi Gong (Chi Kung), which named him the Qi Gong Master of the Year.

The Universal Tao System and Training Center

THE UNIVERSAL TAO SYSTEM

The ultimate goal of Taoist practice is to transcend physical boundaries through the development of the soul and the spirit within the human. That is also the guiding principle behind the Universal Tao, a practical system of self-development that enables individuals to complete the harmonious evolution of their physical, mental, and spiritual bodies. Through a series of ancient Chinese meditative and internal energy exercises, the practitioner learns to increase physical energy, release tension, improve health, practice self-defense, and gain the ability to heal oneself and others. In the process of creating a solid foundation of health and well-being in the physical body, the practitioner also creates the basis for developing his or her spiritual potential by learning to tap into the natural energies of the sun, moon, earth, stars, and other environmental forces.

The Universal Tao practices are derived from ancient techniques rooted in the processes of nature. They have been gathered and integrated into a coherent, accessible system for well-being that works directly with the life force, or Chi, that flows through the meridian system of the body.

Master Chia has spent years developing and perfecting techniques for teaching these traditional practices to students around the world through ongoing classes, workshops, private instruction, and healing sessions, as well as books and video and audio products. Further information can be obtained at www.universal-tao.com.

THE UNIVERSAL TAO TRAINING CENTER

The Tao Garden Health Spa and Resort in northern Thailand is the home of Master Chia and serves as the worldwide headquarters for Universal Tao activities. This integrated wellness, holistic health, and training center is situated on eighty acres surrounded by the beautiful Himalayan foothills near the historic walled city of Chiang Mai. The serene setting includes flower and herb gardens ideal for meditation, open-air pavilions for practicing Chi Kung, and a health and fitness spa.

The Center offers classes year-round, as well as summer and winter retreats. It can accommodate two hundred students, and group leasing can be arranged. For more information, you may fax the Center at (66) (53) 495-852, or email ip@universal-tao.com.

 *Index*

BOOKS OF RELATED INTEREST

Taoist Cosmic Healing
Chi Kung Color Healing Principles for
Detoxification and Rejuvenation
by Mantak Chia

Taoist Astral Healing
Chi Kung Healing Practices Using Star and Planet Energies
by Mantak Chia and Dirk Oellibrandt

Sexual Reflexology
Activating the Taoist Points of Love
by Mantak Chia and William U. Wei

Golden Elixir Chi Kung
by Mantak Chia

The Jade Emperor's Mind Seal Classic
The Taoist Guide to Health, Longevity, and Immortality
by Stuart Alve Olson

Qigong Teachings of a Taoist Immortal
The Eight Essential Exercises of Master Li Ching-yun
by Stuart Alve Olson

Nei Kung
The Secret Teachings of the Warrior Sages
by Kosta Danaos

Martial Arts Teaching Tales of Power and Paradox
Freeing the Mind, Focusing Chi, and Mastering the Self
by Pascal Fauliot

INNER TRADITIONS • BEAR & COMPANY
P.O. Box 388
Rochester, VT 05767
1-800-246-8648
www.InnerTraditions.com

Or contact your local bookseller